Python Made Simple

The Easy Way to Learn Programming

Learn Python from zero: Clearly, confidently, and the way you actually understand

Dr. Pooja Dubey
Doctorate HRM, B.E. ETC. PGDM Marketing

notionpress.com
INDIA • SINGAPORE • MALAYSIA

ISBN
Paperback 979-8-90296-823-8
Hardcase 979-8-90342-671-3

Author: Dr. Pooja Dubey

Title: Python Made Simple: The Easy Way to Learn Programming

First Edition: 2026

Dedication

To my dad, mom, and every learner who ever felt that programming was *"not for them."* To the curious minds who believe learning should be simple, visual, and human. And to those who dare to start—even when the path feels unfamiliar.

This book is for you.

Acknowledgements

This book would not exist without the journey that shaped it.

I would like to acknowledge the learners, professionals, and colleagues who continuously inspired me to simplify complexity and make learning accessible. My experiences across learning design, facilitation, and content creation over the years reinforced one belief—**learning works best when it feels clear, relatable, and empowering.**

I am grateful to the evolving world of technology and artificial intelligence, which sparked my curiosity, challenged my thinking, and pushed me to learn continuously. The opportunity to explore AI through action-based learning played a significant role in motivating me to dive deeper into Python and application building.

Finally, my gratitude goes to every self-learner who proves that growth begins with curiosity and persistence.

Preface

This book did not begin as a book.

It began as **notes**.

I was trying to self-teach Python—slowly, carefully, and honestly. Like many beginners, I wasn't struggling with intelligence or effort. I was struggling with **how programming was explained**.

As a learning and development professional, I naturally found myself simplifying concepts, breaking them down, and re-explaining them in my own words.

Over time, those notes turned into **visual explanations**, slides, and structured learning material.

With **18 years of experience as a trainer, developer, content creator and L&D professional**, I have always believed that learning should:

- Reduce fear
- Build confidence
- Respect the learner's pace

As an **AI enthusiast** and a **Doctorate in Learning and Development**, my curiosity deepened further when I underwent **AI training as part of action-based learning**.

That experience opened a new door—not just into AI, but into understanding how Python acts as a bridge between human thinking and intelligent systems.

This book is the result of that journey.

It is not written to impress experts.

It is written to **support beginners**.

You will not find unnecessary jargon here.

You will find explanations, real-life examples, flow thinking, visual metaphors, and structured progression.

If you are someone who:

- Wants to learn Python from scratch
- Thinks visually
- Appreciates clarity over complexity
- Wants to build applications, not just write code

Then this book was written for you.

Inside this Book...

Chapter 1 – Why Python Matters Today

Introduces programming and explains why Python is one of the most relevant and beginner-friendly languages today 13

Chapter 2 – What Is Programming and How Computers Think

Explains how computers process instructions and why logical thinking matters more than syntax 21

Chapter 3 – Understanding Variables in Python

Introduces variables as data containers and explains different data types using real-life examples 39

Chapter 4 – How Python Makes Decisions in Python

Explains decision-making using if–else with practical examples from school, banking, HR, and e-commerce 54

Chapter 5 – Repeating Tasks Using Loops

Introduces for and while loops and shows how repetition powers real systems 67

Chapter 6 – How Python Learns to Make Decisions: Because Real Life doesn't Run in Straight Lines

Strengthens decision logic through deeper real-world scenarios and application thinking 95

Chapter 7 – Function – Teaching Python to Do One Job at a Time: Because Good Programs are Built Step by Step, not all at Once

Connects all fundamentals to real applications, introduces flow thinking and user logic 119

Chapter 8 – Putting It All Together: How Real Programs are Built

Demonstrates how variables, decisions, loops, and structure work together to form complete programs 141

Chapter 9 – Working with Group Data: List of Information

Introduces file structure, modular thinking, and how professional applications are organized 161

Chapter 10 – Reading & Writing Files: Taking Python Data to the Real World

Explains file handling, data persistence, and real-world corporate data processing 171

Chapter 11 – AI-Assisted Coding: How Python Learners Can Work Smarter

Introduces AI tools like Cursor and Google environments, showing how modern developers work with AI 187

Chapter 12 – Python Programming Wrap-Up

A reflective conclusion that focuses on mindset, growth, and career direction as an application builder 199

Answer Key & Solutions

Detailed answers, explanations, case study solutions for assessments and exercises 209

Chapter 1

Why Python Matters Today

1.1 Understanding the World of Programming

We live in a world powered by computers. From smartphones and laptops to ATMs, traffic signals, and online shopping apps—computers are everywhere. But have you ever wondered how these machines know what to do?

A computer does not think like a human. It does not guess, assume, or understand emotions. It only follows **instructions**, and it follows them **exactly** in the order they are given.

This set of instructions given to a computer is called a **program**, and the act of writing these instructions is called **programming**.

Think of programming like giving directions to someone who understands only one language. If your instructions are unclear or out of order, the task will fail. Computers are even stricter than humans—they do not correct your mistakes.

That is why programming languages exist. They help humans talk to computers in a structured, logical, and predictable way.

Among all programming languages available today, Python stands out as one of the easiest and most powerful ways to begin this conversation with a computer.

Industry surveys also show that Python is especially popular among new programmers, with many learners using it as their first language because of its readable, English-like syntax and gentle learning curve. For example, in the 2025 Python Developer Survey, a large portion of users reported being relatively new to programming, which reflects Python's approachability for beginners.

1.2 Why Python is so important

Python is a programming language that was designed with **simplicity** in mind. Its goal is to help people focus on *solving problems* rather than struggling with complicated syntax.

Many beginners fear programming because they think it is full of difficult symbols and confusing rules. Python removes much of that fear. It looks almost like normal English.

For example, reading a Python program often feels like reading simple instructions rather than complex code.

This simplicity makes Python extremely important today because:

- More people want to learn programming
- Technology is entering every field
- Companies need solutions faster than ever

Python allows people from **non-technical backgrounds**—students, teachers, business professionals, analysts—to use programming without spending years learning complex rules.

That is why Python is often recommended as the **first programming language** for beginners.

Python is not just easy—it is also extremely powerful. It is used in many real-life applications that we interact with every day.

Here are some common areas where Python is used:

1. Web Applications

Popular websites and platforms use Python behind the scenes to manage data, users, and content.

2. Data Analysis and Data Science

Python is widely used to analyze large amounts of data—such as sales reports, exam results, customer behavior, and business trends.

3. Artificial Intelligence and Machine Learning

Python helps machines learn from data, recognize patterns, and make decisions. This powers features like recommendations, voice assistants, and image recognition.

4. Automation

Python can automate repetitive tasks such as:

- Sending emails
- Processing files
- Managing records

This saves time and reduces human error.

5. Education

Schools and colleges across India now teach Python because it helps students understand logic and problem-solving.

Because Python can be used in **so many fields**, learning it opens doors to multiple opportunities.

1.3 Why Python is so popular

Python's popularity has grown rapidly over the last decade. One major reason is its **community**.

Python has:

- Millions of users worldwide
- Huge collections of ready-made tools (libraries)
- Strong support from companies and universities

This means if you get stuck, help is easily available. You don't have to build everything from scratch. You can learn faster using examples created by others

Another reason for Python's popularity is that it works across platforms. The same Python program can run on Windows, macOS, and Linux

This flexibility makes Python suitable for both small projects and large enterprise systems.

Python has become one of the **most in-demand skills** in the Indian job market.

Python is widely used in:

- IT companies
- Startups
- Banks and finance companies
- EdTech platforms
- Research and analytics firms

Some common job roles that use Python include:

- Software Developer
- Data Analyst
- Data Scientist
- Automation Engineer
- Business Analyst

Even students preparing for careers in engineering, commerce, science, or management benefit from learning Python because it strengthens logical thinking and problem-solving skills.

In India, Python is also popular because:

- It is taught in CBSE and ICSE schools
- Many universities include it in their syllabus
- Online learning platforms focus heavily on Python

Learning Python today is not just about coding—it is about preparing for a **future-ready career**.

Key Takeaways

- Programming means giving step-by-step instructions to a computer.
- Computers follow instructions exactly and do not guess.
- Python is a programming language designed to be simple and readable.
- Python is used in web development, data analysis, automation, and AI.
- Python's popularity comes from its simplicity, flexibility, and strong community.
- Learning Python improves logical thinking and career opportunities.
- Python has strong career scope in India for students and professionals.

1. Let's check your understanding

1A. Multiple Choice Questions

1. What is programming?

   a) Teaching computers emotions

   b) Giving instructions to computers

   c) Using the internet

   d) Playing games

2. Why is Python considered beginner-friendly?

   a) It uses complex symbols

   b) It looks similar to English

   c) It works only on one system

   d) It is slow

3. Which of the following is NOT a use of Python?

   a) Web development

   b) Data analysis

   c) Automation

   d) Hardware manufacturing

4. Why is Python popular in India?

   a) It is expensive

   b) It is difficult

   c) It is taught in schools and colleges

   d) It is outdated

1B. Short Answer Questions

5. Explain in your own words what programming means.
6. List any two applications of Python.
7. Why is Python useful for students?

1.C Thinking Exercise

8. Write one real-life task that you think Python could help automate.

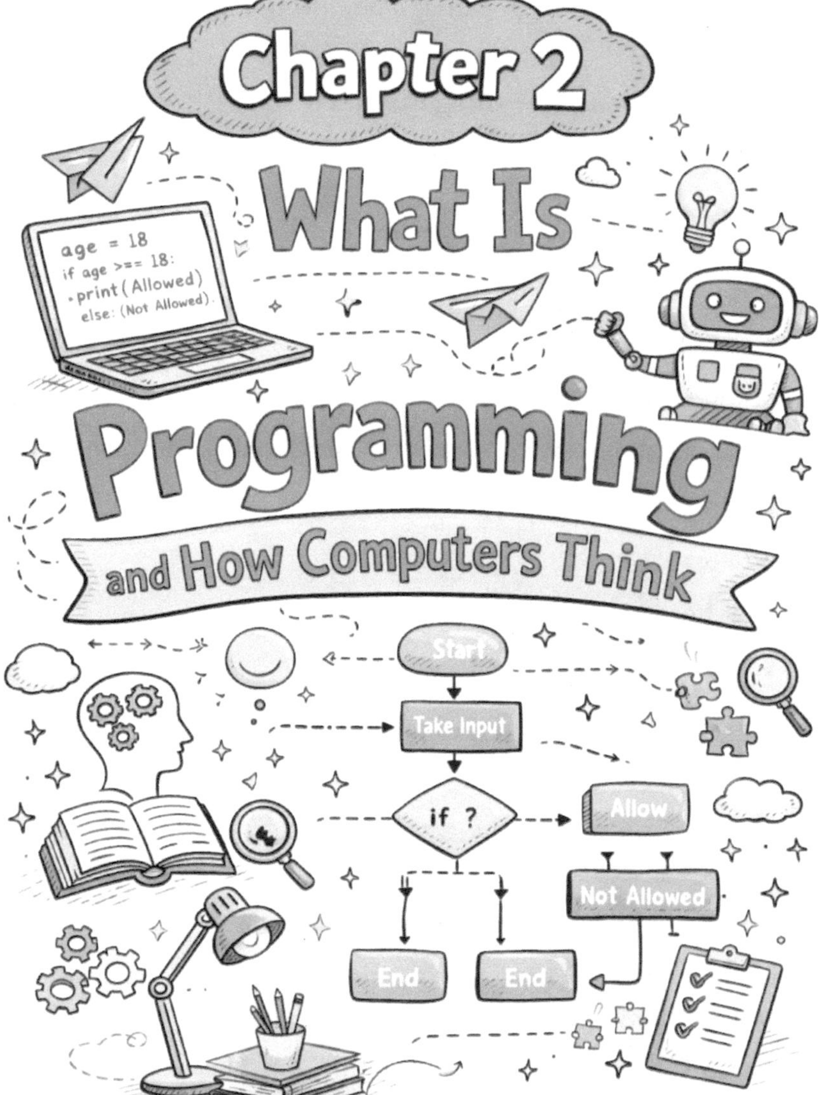
Chapter 2
What Is
Programming
and How Computers Think
age = 18
if age >== 18:
• print (Allowed)
else: (Not Allowed).
Start
Take Input
if ?
Allow
Not Allowed
End
End

2.1 What Can a Computer Really Do?

Many beginners think computers are "smart." In reality, computers are not intelligent in the human sense. They do not think, understand, or decide on their own.

A computer can do only **one thing extremely well**:

☞ **Follow instructions exactly as written, in the exact order, without guessing.**

If you tell a human, *"Make tea,"* they will automatically understand many hidden steps.

A computer cannot do that.

A computer needs **very clear, step-by-step instructions**.

For example, instead of saying *"Make tea"*, instructions must look like this:

- Take a cup
- Add tea leaves
- Pour hot water
- Wait for 3 minutes
- Remove tea leaves

This complete set of instructions is called a **program**.

Programming is simply the act of breaking a task into **small, clear steps** that a computer can follow.

Programming Is Like Giving Precise Directions

Think about meeting someone for the first time. You talk, get along well, and want to contact them again later.

What do you do? You **save their name and phone number** in your mobile phone.

Your phone stores information like this:

- Name → John
- Mobile Number → 9966445531

In programming, we do the same thing.

We store information so that the computer can remember and use it later. This stored information is called **data**, and the containers that hold this data are called **variables.**

Programming is not magic.

It is simply:

- Storing information
- Giving instructions
- Asking the computer to act on that information

Once you understand this, programming becomes much less scary.

2.2 How Python Helps Us Talk to Computers

Python is a programming language that helps humans communicate with computers in a **simple and readable way**.

Let us look at how Python stores information.

Suppose you want to store a person's name.

In Python, you can write:

name = "John"

Here:

- name is the variable
- "John" is the value stored in it

The = sign does not mean "equals" like in mathematics.

It means **"store this value inside this name."**

Python uses **quotes** (" ") for text.

This text is called a **string**.

So when you see:

```
name = "John"
```

You should read it as:

Store the text *John* inside the variable *name*

This is how Python starts making sense of the world.

2.3 Why Order and Accuracy Matter in Programming

One important rule in programming is this:

☞ **Order matters. Accuracy matters even more.**

If you change the order of instructions, the result may change.

If you make a small mistake, the computer will not "fix it for you."

For example:

- Misspelling a word
- Forgetting quotes
- Writing instructions in the wrong order

Python will not guess your intention.

It will either:

- Do exactly what you wrote
- Or stop with an error

This may feel strict at first, but it is actually a good thing. It forces you to think clearly and logically.

Over time, this improves:

- Problem-solving skills
- Attention to detail
- Logical thinking

2.4 Programming Is Thinking Clearly

At its core, programming is **thinking before typing**.

Before writing code, you should ask:

- What is the task?
- What information is needed?
- What steps are required?
- In what order should they happen?

Python encourages this way of thinking because it removes unnecessary complexity.

Let us understand this using **two practical examples**—one from daily life and one from the real world of work.

Example 1: Ordering Food Online

What is the task?

The task is to order food using a food delivery app.

What information is needed?

- Restaurant name
- Food items
- Delivery address
- Payment method

What steps are required?

- Open the food delivery app
- Select a restaurant
- Choose food items
- Add items to cart
- Enter delivery address
- Make payment

In what order should they happen?

The order is extremely important.

You cannot pay **before** selecting food, and you cannot select food **before** opening the app.

If the order is wrong, the task fails—just like a computer program.

This is exactly how a computer thinks:

task → data → steps → correct order

Example 2: From the World of Work – Employee Attendance System

Now let's look at a real-world professional example.

Suppose you work in an office and your company wants to build a simple system to check whether an employee is allowed entry.

What is the task?

Check if an employee should be marked *Present* or *Absent.*

What information is needed?

- Employee ID
- Login time
- Office start time

What steps are required?

- Get the employee's login time
- Compare login time with office start time
- Decide status (Present or Late)
- Store the result

In what order should they happen?

The system **must first collect data**, then **compare**, and only then **decide**.

If the decision is made before checking the login time, the system becomes useless.

This is how real software systems in offices, banks, schools, and companies are designed—by breaking problems into **clear, logical steps**.

Why This Matters in Python

Python programming follows this same thinking style.

Before writing even one line of code, you should train yourself to think like this:

"What exactly am I trying to do, what data do I need, and what is the correct order of steps?"

When you do this:

- Your programs become simpler
- Errors reduce drastically
- Debugging becomes easier
- Your thinking becomes structured

This is why learning Python is not just about coding—it is about learning **how to think clearly and logically**.

You don't need to memorize hundreds of rules to get started.

You just need to:

- Think clearly
- Write simple instructions
- Let the computer do the work

This is why Python is such a powerful language for beginners—it trains your mind to think logically while keeping the learning process simple.

Why Planning Matters

Imagine writing the code **without planning**:

- What if you forget the marks?
- What if you check the condition before storing marks?
- What if you try to print the result without deciding?

The program would fail.

That is why **good programmers plan before coding**, just like we did using:

- Task
- Information
- Steps
- Order

Key Learning

When you learn Python, you are really learning how to:

- Break problems into small parts
- Think step by step
- Communicate clearly with a computer

This skill is useful not only in programming but also in:

- Office work
- Project planning
- Decision making
- Problem solving in daily life

2.5 From Planning to Python Logic

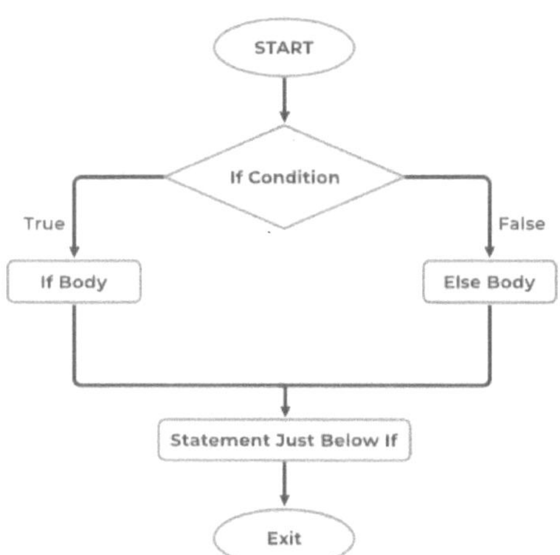

Real-World Work Example: Office Entry System

Imagine you are working in a bar that uses software to decide whether a guest is **Allowed** or **Not Allowed** inside.

What is the task?

Decide whether a guest can enter the pub.

What information is needed?

- guest age

What steps are required?

- Check the age
- Compare it with bar policy
- Decide entry status

In what order should they happen?

Decision must be made **after** checking the age.

How a Human Thinks

If age is 18 or more → Allow entry

Else → Do not allow

```
age = 19
if age >= 18:
    print("Allowed")
else:
    print("Not Allowed")
```

Python is not deciding anything on its own.

It is only following **your instructions in the correct order**.

2.6 From Thinking to Code: A Simple Python-Style Example

Let us now convert the four planning questions into a **Python-style example**, without worrying about advanced syntax.

Problem: Check if a Student Has Passed an Exam

What is the task? Check whether a student has **passed or failed** an exam.

What information is needed?

- Marks obtained by the student
- Passing marks (let's assume 40)

What steps are required?

- Take the student's marks
- Compare it with passing marks
- Decide the result (Pass or Fail)
- Show the result

In what order should they happen?

Marks must be checked **before** deciding the result.

Decision must be made **before** showing output.

How a Human Thinks (Logic First)

A human naturally thinks like this:

If marks are 40 or more → Pass

Otherwise → Fail

How Python Thinks

```
marks = 50

if marks >= 40:
```

```
    print("Pass")
else:
    print("Fail")
```

Let's break this down:

marks = 50 → Store the marks

if marks >= 40: → Check the condition

print("Pass") → Show result if condition is true

else: → What to do if condition is false

Python is **not doing anything magical** here. It is simply following the steps **in order**, exactly as planned.

Let us try a Workplace Data Flow and do some real Software Thinking. This same thinking pattern is used in:

- Attendance systems
- Online exams
- Banking transactions
- School result systems
- HR and payroll software

Every real software system starts with:

- Define the task
- Collect required data
- Process step by step
- Follow the correct order

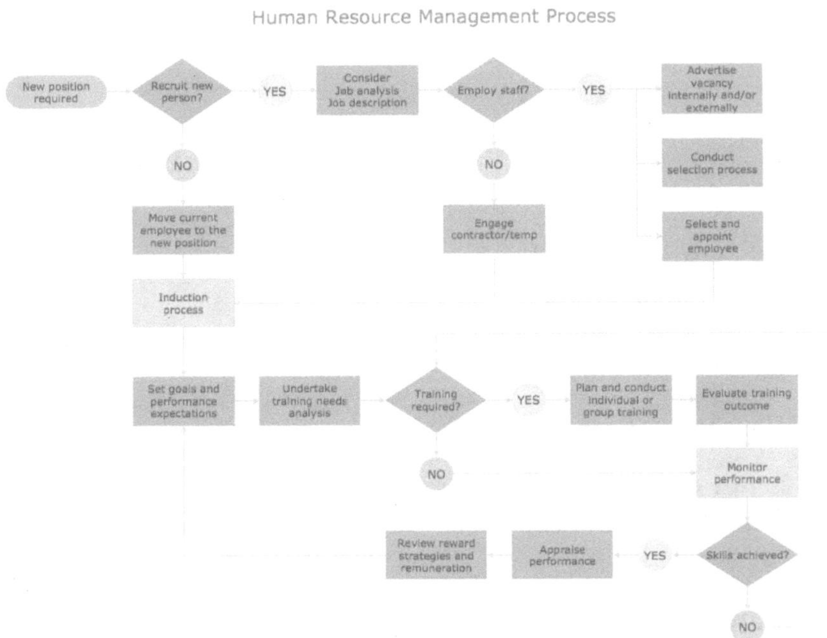

Can you try to understand this?

An **Employee Management System** is software used by companies to manage employee-related decisions such as attendance, access, salary, training, and compliance.

Let's understand a **simple flow diagram** that decides whether an employee is **Allowed** or **Not Allowed** based on company rules.

Step 1: Start the Process

Every system begins with a **start point**. This means:

- An employee is trying to log in
- Or an employee is entering the office
- Or HR is checking employee details

In programming, this is where the program **starts running**.

Step 2: Collect Employee Data (Input)

The system first **collects information** about the employee.

For example:

- Employee ID
- Age
- Role
- Login time

☞ **Why this is important:**

A system **cannot make decisions without data**. In Python, this would mean storing values in variables.

Step 3: Apply Company Rules (Decision Point)

Now the system checks the company policy.

Example rule:

If employee role is listed, allow access. Otherwise, deny access

This is shown in the flow diagram as a **diamond shape**, which always means:

☞ **A decision has to be made**

In programming terms, this is an **if–else condition**.

Step 4: Yes/No Branching (Logic Path)

From the decision point, the flow splits into two paths:

Yes Path (Condition True)

- Employee meets the requirement
- Action: **Allow**
- Status is stored or displayed

No Path (Condition False)

- Employee does not meet the requirement
- Action: **Not Allowed**
- System may show a warning or message

This branching is very important because:

- Computers never do both actions
- They choose **only one path** based on the condition

Step 5: Output (Result Shown)

Finally, the system shows the result:

"Allowed" or "Not Allowed"

This is the **output** of the system.

In Python, this is usually done using the print() statement.

Why Python Makes This Easy

Python encourages this thinking because:

- It reads like plain English
- It forces clear structure
- It avoids unnecessary complexity

That is why Python is taught in schools, colleges, and used in companies—it trains you to think logically **before** writing code.

How This Looks in Python Thinking:

```
login_time = 10

if login_time <= 10:
    print("Allowed")
else:
    print("Not Allowed")
```

Python follows the flow diagram exactly:

- Start
- Read data

- Check condition
- Choose path
- Show result

Why This Flow Diagram Is Important

This same flow structure is used in:

- Attendance systems
- Online exams
- Banking transactions
- HR onboarding systems
- Payroll and salary processing

Once you understand flow diagrams, programming becomes easier because:

- You already know what the code should do
- You just need to write it in Python

Key Message for you

If you can explain a task clearly to another human, you can explain it to Python.

Once you master this way of thinking, programming stops being difficult and starts becoming **logical and predictable**.

Flow diagrams are visual plans for programs.

Python is just a way to write those plans in a language the computer understands.

If you can read a flow diagram, you can **write code confidently**.

Key Takeaways

- Computers do not think; they only follow instructions.
- A program is a set of step-by-step instructions.
- Programming means breaking tasks into small, clear steps.
- Python helps humans talk to computers using simple, readable code.
- Variables are used to store information.
- Text values in Python are written inside quotes.
- Order and accuracy are extremely important in programming.
- Programming improves logical and structured thinking.

Let's check your understanding

Note: *Answers to all assessment questions are provided at the end of the book.*

2A. Multiple Choice Questions

1. What is a program?

   a) A computer device

   b) A set of instructions

   c) A mobile app

   d) A calculation

2. Why can't a computer understand "Make tea"?

   a) It is vague

   b) It does not understand tea

   c) It needs exact step-by-step instructions

   d) It cannot boil water

3. What does the = sign mean in Python?

   a) Equals

   b) Compare

   c) Store a value

   d) Print

4. Why are quotes used in Python?

   a) To show numbers

   b) To show commands

   c) To store text

   d) To end a program

2B. Short Answer Questions

- Explain why computers cannot guess instructions.
- What is a variable? Explain using a real-life example.
- Why is Python good for beginners?

2C. Thinking Exercise:

Write step-by-step instructions for making a sandwich as if you were explaining it to a computer.

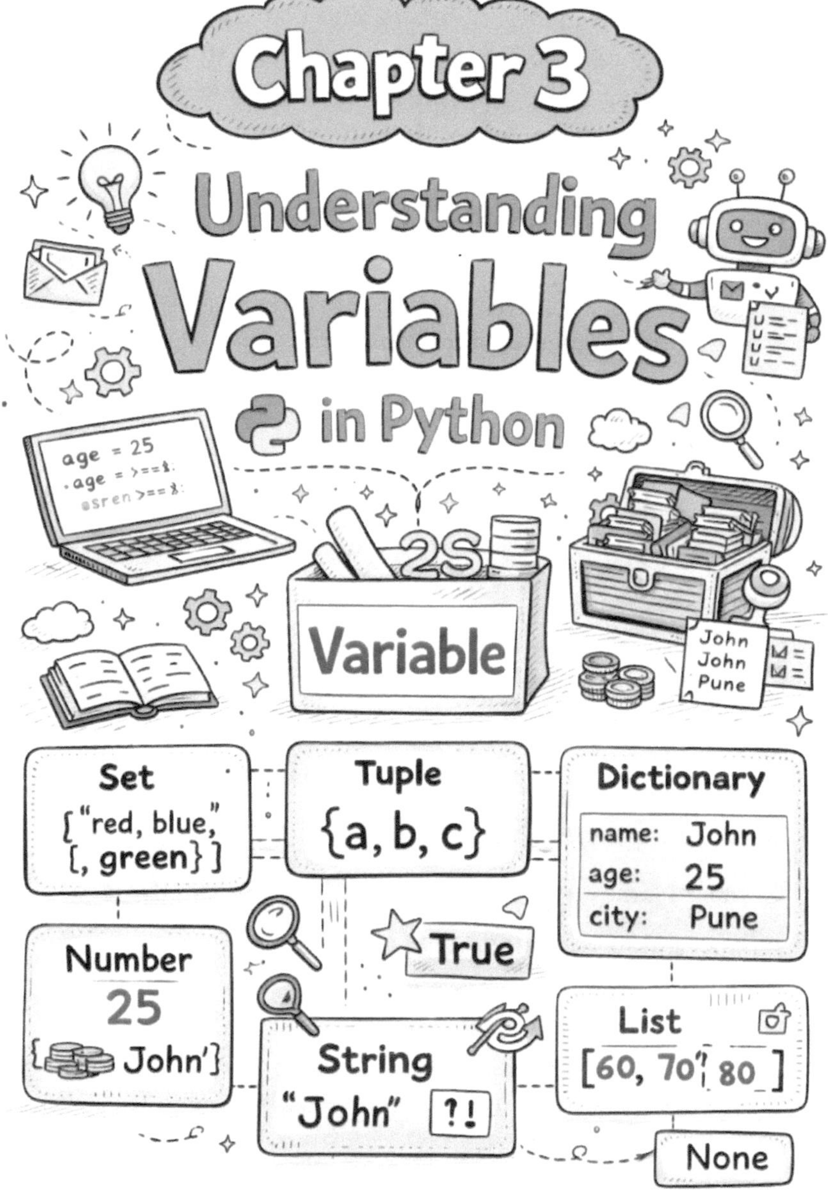
Chapter 3
Understanding
Variables
in Python
age = 25
Variable
John
John
Pune
Set
["red, blue,"
[, green}]
Tuple
{a, b, c}
Dictionary
name: John
age: 25
city: Pune
True
Number
25
John'}
String
"John"
?!
List
[60, 70, 80]
None

3.1 What Are Variables?

In programming, computers need a way to **remember information**. Just like humans remember names, numbers, and places, computers also store information so they can use it later. In Python, this stored information is kept inside something called a **variable**. The easiest way to understand a variable is to think of it as: **A box that stores something, and this box has a name.**

For example:

- A box named age can store your age
- A box named name can store your name

If your age is 25, Python stores it like this:

age = 25

Here:

- age is the **variable name**
- 25 is the **value**
- = means **store this value inside this variable**

Once stored, Python remembers it until the program ends. We use variables in real life all the time without realizing it.

Think about your phone contacts:

- Contact Name → John
- Phone Number → 9955667741

Your phone stores this information so you don't have to remember it every time.

Python does the same thing.

```
name = "John"
city = "Pune"
company = "Talmond"
```

Each line stores one piece of information.

☞ **Important Rule:** Python uses **quotes (" ") for text**, also called **strings**.

So:

- "John" is text
- 25 is a number

Mixing them incorrectly will confuse Python.

3.2 Types of Variables in Python

Python supports different types of data. Let's look at the most common ones beginners use.

1. Numbers

Used to store numeric values.

```
age = 25
price = 22.5
```

Whole numbers → int

Decimal numbers → float

2. Text (Strings)

Used to store words or sentences.

```
name = "John"
state = "Gujarat"
```

Strings must always be inside quotes.

3. Boolean Values

Used when something is either **True or False.**

```
is_adult = True
is_logged_in = False
```

Boolean values are very useful for decisions.

These are basic types of variables but when you advance in your career, you might learn more specialized types that we are leaving for now as you are just starting out.

We don't want to make this complicated for you.

Variable Naming Rules (Very Important)

Python follows some strict rules when naming variables.

1. Variables are case-sensitive

This means:

```
name = "John"
Name = "Amit"
```

These are **two different variables.**

2. Use lowercase letters

By convention, Python variables are written in lowercase.

```
age = 25    # correct
Age = 25    # not recommended
```

3. Use meaningful names

Bad variable names:

```
x = 25
y = "John"
```

Good variable names:

```
age = 25
name = "John"
```

Good names make programs easier to read and understand.

Variables make programs:

- Flexible
- Reusable
- Easy to update

Imagine writing a program without variables. You would have to rewrite everything every time data changes.

For example, instead of writing age directly inside decisions, we store it:

```
age = 19

if age >= 18:
    print("Allowed")
else:
    print("Not Allowed")
```

Now if the age changes, you only change **one line**.

This is why variables are the **foundation of all programs**.

Without variables:

- No user data
- No decisions
- No real applications

3.3 Other Types of Variables in Python (Advanced Overview)

Important Note for the learner

⚠ **Note for Beginners:**

The next section introduces **advanced types of variables** used in Python.

If this feels confusing on your first read, **you can safely skip this section** and come back to it later.

Understanding basic variables (numbers, text, True/False) is enough to continue learning Python.

This section is included to give you **early exposure**, not pressure.

So far, you have learned about:

- Numbers
- Strings (text)
- Boolean values

Python, however, can store **much more complex data**, especially when working with real-world applications. Let's look at other important types of variables you mentioned in your slides.

1. Sequence Types – Storing Multiple Values

a) List

A **list** stores many values in one variable.

```
marks = [60, 70, 65, 80, 90]
```

- Uses square brackets [ ]
- Values are ordered
- Values can be changed later

Lists are used for:

- Marks of students
- Orders of a customer
- Names of users

☞ You'll study lists in detail in a later chapter.

b) Tuple

A **tuple** is similar to a list, but its values **cannot be changed.**

```
coordinates = (10, 20)
```

- Uses round brackets ( )
- Used when data should remain fixed

Example use:

- Location coordinates
- Fixed configuration values

c) Range

A **range** represents a sequence of numbers.

```
numbers = range(1, 6)
```

This represents:

1, 2, 3, 4, 5

Ranges are commonly used in loops.

2. Mapping Type – Dictionary

A **dictionary** stores data in **label–value pairs**.

```
student = {
    "name": "John",
    "age": 15,
    "city": "Pune"
}
```

Think of it like a real dictionary:

- Word → Meaning
- Label → Value

Dictionaries are used heavily in:

- User profiles
- Employee records
- Application data

☞ You will explore dictionaries deeply in later chapters.

3. Set Types – Unique Values Only

A **set** stores **unique values.**

```
colors = {"red", "blue", "green"}
```

- Duplicate values are automatically removed
- Order does not matter

Used when:

- You don't want repeated data
- You want to compare groups

There is also a **frozenset**, which is a fixed (unchangeable) version of a set.

4. Binary Types – Working with Files and Data

These types are used when Python works with:

- Images
- Videos
- Files
- Network data

Example

```
data = b"Hello"
```

Types include:

- bytes
- bytearray
- memoryview

☞ These are **advanced-level topics** and not required for beginners.

5. NoneType – When There Is No Value

Sometimes a variable exists but has **no value yet.**

```
result = None
```

This means:

"Nothing is stored here right now."

Used when: Waiting for user input

> **"The Quiet Builder"**
>
> **EXERCISE: MAKING SPACE FOR INFORMATION**
>
> In real applications, programs often prepare variables long before they receive actual data.
>
> **YOUR TASK**
>
> Write Python variables to store the following details:
>
> - A learner's name
> - A learner's email address
> - A learner's country
>
> Do not assign any value yet—only create placeholders.

Value will be calculated later. This is very common in real applications.

Why Python Has So Many Variable Types

Python supports many variable types because **real life is complex.** Different situations need different ways of storing data:

- One value → number or string
- Many values → list or tuple
- Labelled data → dictionary
- Unique data → set

The good news is: You do **not** need to master all of them at once. Python lets you learn **step by step**.

What Beginners Should Focus On First

- Numbers
- Strings
- Boolean values
- Lists (later chapter)
- Dictionaries (later chapter)

Everything else can wait.

Key Takeaways

- Variables store data in Python.
- Different data needs different variable types.
- Numbers, strings, and Booleans are the most important for beginners.
- Lists store multiple values.
- Dictionaries store labelled data.
- Sets store unique values.
- Some variable types are advanced and can be skipped initially.
- Python allows learning gradually without pressure.

Let's check your understanding

Note: *Answers to all questions are provided at the end of the book.*

3A. Beginner-Level Assessment

1. What is a variable in Python?

   a) A loop

   b) A condition

   c) A box that stores data

   d) A function

2. What does the = symbol mean in Python?

   a) Compare two values

   b) Assign a value to a variable

   c) Print output

   d) End a program

3. Which of the following is a string?

   a) 25

   b) 3.14

   c) "Python"

   d) True

4. Which variable name is recommended in Python?

   a) Age

   b) student name

   c) student_name

   d) 1student

5. Python variables are:

   a) Not case-sensitive

   b) Case-sensitive

   c) Always uppercase

   d) Only numeric

Short Answer Questions

6. Explain what a variable is using a real-life example.
7. Why do strings need quotes in Python?
8. What is the difference between name and Name in Python?

Practical Exercise

9. Write Python code to store:
   - Your name
   - Your age
   - Whether you are a student (True/False)

3B. Intermediate-Level Assessment

10. Identify the type of variable:

    a) marks = [60, 70, 80]

    b) price = 22.5

    c) is_logged_in = False

    d) city = "Delhi"

11. What will happen if you write:

    age = "25"

    a) Python will give an error

    b) Age will be stored as a number

    c) Age will be stored as text

    d) Python will ignore it

Why are meaningful variable names important?

(Write any two reasons.)

3C. Advanced-Level Assessment (Optional)

⚠ *This section is for learners who explored advanced variable types.*

Beginners may skip this section on first reading.

12. Which data type stores values in label–value pairs?

    a) List

    b) Tuple

    c) Dictionary

    d) Set

13. Which of the following stores only unique values?

    a) List

    b) Tuple

    c) Dictionary

    d) Set

14. Which data type cannot be changed after creation?

    a) List

    b) Tuple

    c) Dictionary

    d) Set

15. What does the following represent?

    result = None

    a) Zero value

    b) Empty string

    c) No value assigned yet

    d) Error

Short Answer Questions

16. Write one real-world example where a dictionary would be useful.
17. What is the difference between a list and a tuple?

Thinking Exercise

18. You are storing details of an employee:

- Name
- Age
- Department

Which variable type would you use and why?

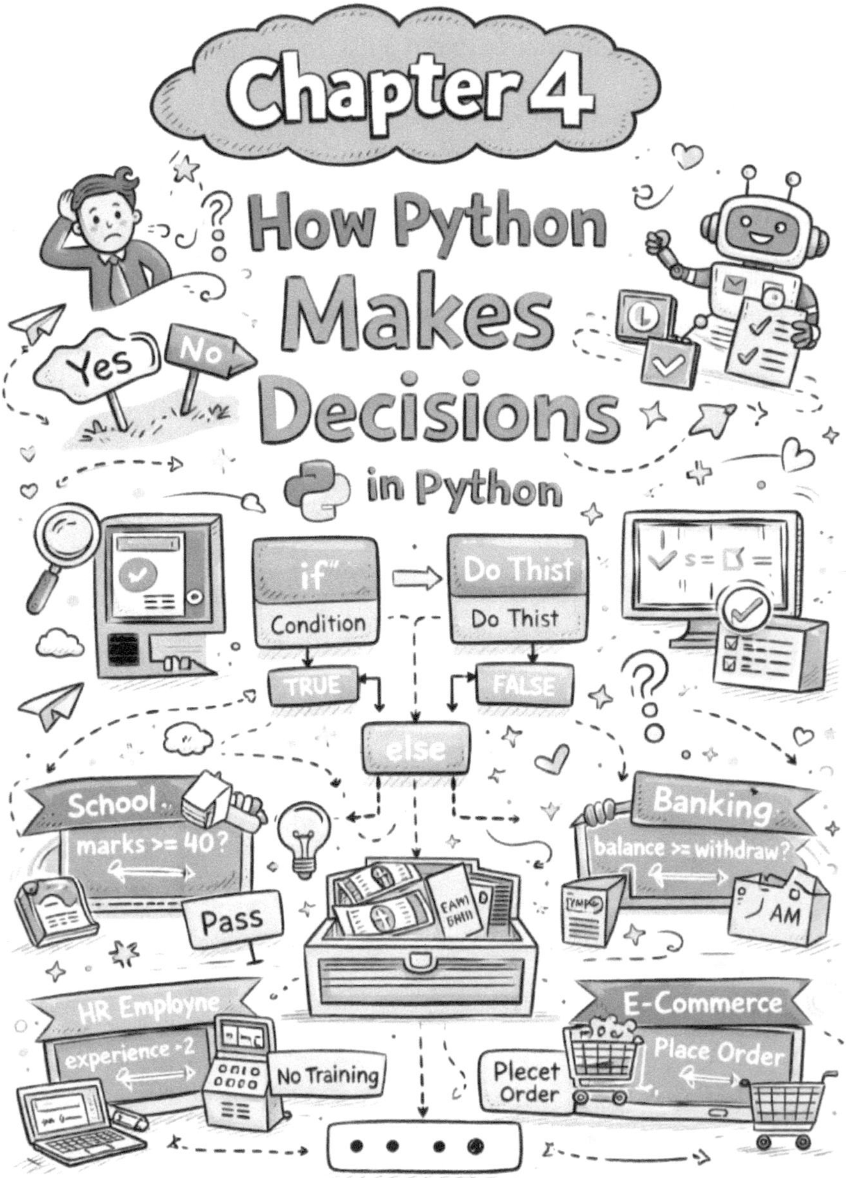
Chapter 4
How Python Makes Decisions
in Python
Yes
No
if"
Condition
Do Thist
Do Thist
TRUE
FALSE
else
School
marks >= 40?
Pass
Banking
balance >= withdraw?
AM
HR Employne
No Training
E-Commerce
Place Order
Plecet Order

4.1 Why Decisions Matter in Programming

In real life, we make decisions all the time.

- If it is raining, we take an umbrella
- If traffic is high, we leave early
- If we are hungry, we eat

Computers also need to make decisions. But unlike humans, computers **cannot decide on their own**. They need **clear rules.** In Python, decisions are made using:

- if
- else

These words tell Python:

- What to check
- What to do if the condition is true
- What to do if the condition is false

Let's start with a very simple example.

Life Situation: Is It Raining?

Logic:

- If it is raining → Take an umbrella

Python Code:

```
is_raining = True

if is_raining:
    print("Take Umbrella")
```

What is happening here?

is_raining = True → Store the condition

if is_raining: → Check if the condition is true

print("Take Umbrella") → Action taken

☞ Python checks the condition.

If it is **True**, the instruction runs.

If it is **False**, Python skips it.

if–else can also be used for Two-Way Decisions

Most real decisions have **two outcomes**.

Example: Guest Entry in a Club

Rule:

- If age is 18 or more → Allowed
- Else → Not Allowed

Python Code:

```
age = 19

if age >= 18:
    print("Allowed")
else:
    print("Not Allowed")
```

Key things to notice:

>= means "greater than or equal to"

: is required after if and else

Indentation (spaces) shows which code belongs together

☞ **Indentation is very important in Python**

Python uses indentation instead of brackets.

Let's take an example based on temperature.

Life Rule:

- If temperature is 25 or more → Hot
- Else → Cold

Python Code:

```
temperature = 19

if temperature >= 25:
    print("Hot")
else:
    print("Cold")
```

Here:

- Python checks the value of temperature
- Makes a decision
- Prints the result

This is how weather apps, sensors, and monitoring systems work internally.

4.2 Decisions in Software Programming

Decision-making is used everywhere in real software:

➔ **Schools:**

If marks ≥ 40 → Pass, else → Fail

Real-Life Situation

In schools, students are evaluated based on marks.

Rule:

- If marks are **40 or more** → Pass
- Else → Fail

How a Human Thinks

A teacher looks at the marks and decides the result.

How a Computer Thinks

The computer:

- Takes the marks as input
- Checks the condition
- Decides the result

Python Logic

```
marks = 55

if marks >= 40:
    print("Pass")
else:
    print("Fail")
```

☞ This logic is used in:

- Exam result systems
- Online tests

School report card software

> **"The Quiet Builder"**
>
> **EXERCISE: DECIDING ELIGIBILITY**
>
> Not every action in a program happens automatically—some require conditions to be met.
>
> **YOUR TASK**
>
> Write a Python function that:
>
> - Accepts one input indicating whether a learner has completed a task

- Returns True if the task is completed
- Returns False otherwise

➔ **Banking:**

If balance ≥ amount → Allow withdrawal

Real-Life Situation

When you withdraw money from an ATM, the bank checks your balance.

Rule:

If balance is **greater than or equal to withdrawal amount** → Allow withdrawal

- Else → Decline transaction

How a Human Thinks

"Do I have enough money in my account?"

How a Computer Thinks

- Reads account balance
- Reads withdrawal amount
- Compares both
- Takes action

Python Logic

```
balance = 5000


withdraw = 3000
if balance >= withdraw:
    print("Withdrawal Successful")
else:
    print("Insufficient Balance")
```

☞ This logic protects banks from incorrect transactions.

➔ **HR Systems:**

If experience <2 → Training required

Real-Life Situation

Companies often decide whether an employee needs training.

Rule:

- If employee experience is **less than 2 years** → Training required
- Else → No training needed

How a Human Thinks

HR checks how experienced the employee is.

How a Computer Thinks

- Stores experience
- Applies company policy
- Makes a decision

Python Logic

```
experience = 1.5

if experience < 2:
    print("Training Required")
else:
    print("No Training Needed")
```

☞ Used in:

- HR management systems
- Employee onboarding software
- Skill development platforms

➔ **E-commerce:**

If payment successful → Place order

Real-Life Situation

When you place an order online, the system checks payment status.

Rule:

- If payment is successful → Place order
- Else → Cancel order

How a Human Thinks

"Has the payment gone through?"

How a Computer Thinks

- Checks payment status
- Takes action based on result

Python Logic

```
payment_successful = True

if payment_successful:
    print("Order Placed")
else:
    print("Payment Failed")
```

☞ This logic is used in:

- Amazon
- Flipkart
- Food delivery apps
- Ticket booking systems

Python makes decision-making **simple and readable**, which is why it is widely used.

What All These Examples Have in Common

In every case:

- **Data is taken** (marks, balance, age, payment status)
- **Condition is checked**
- **Decision is made**
- **One action is chosen**

This is exactly how if–else works in Python.

Once you understand if–else, you can:

- Control program flow
- Build logic
- Create real-world applications

Key Message for the learner

Every real application you use daily is full of if–else decisions running silently in the background.

Once you understand decision-making in Python, you are one step closer to building **real software**.

Key Takeaways

- Computers cannot think on their own; they make decisions based on rules.
- Python uses if and else statements to make decisions.
- Every decision checks a **condition** that results in True or False.
- If the condition is True, Python executes the if block.
- If the condition is False, Python executes the else block (if present).
- Indentation is mandatory in Python and defines which statements belong together.
- Decision-making is used in real-life systems such as:
- School result systems
- Banking and ATM systems
- HR and employee management systems
- E-commerce and payment systems

Let's check your understanding

Note: *Answers to all assessment questions are provided at the end of the book.*

4A. Multiple Choice Questions

1. Which Python keyword is used to check a condition?

   a) loop

   b) if

   c) print

   d) input

2. What does an if statement do?

   a) Repeats code

   b) Stores data

   c) Makes a decision

   d) Ends a program

3. What must every if condition return?

   a) Number

   b) String

   c) True or False

   d) Output

4. What happens if the if condition is false and there is no else?

   a) Program crashes

   b) Python guesses the output

   c) Nothing happens

   d) Error occurs

5. Why is indentation important in Python?

    a) To improve speed

    b) To decorate code

    c) To define decision blocks

    d) To store values

4B. Short Answer Questions

6. Explain decision-making in Python using a real-life example.
7. What is the role of else in Python?
8. Why do computers need clear rules to make decisions?

4C. Practical Exercises

9. Write a Python program to check:
    - If a person is eligible to vote (age ≥ 18)
10. Write a Python program to check:
    - If a bank account has sufficient balance for withdrawal
11. Write a Python program to check:
    - If a student has passed or failed (passing marks = 40)

Reminder for Learners

- If decision-making feels difficult at first, practice with real-life examples.
- if–else becomes easier when you think in terms of **rules and outcomes.**

Did you know that Python was designed to be read almost like plain English?

Unlike many programming languages that rely heavily on symbols and complex rules, Python focuses on readability and simplicity. This is why beginners often find Python easier to learn—it uses clear words, logical structure, and minimal punctuation.

In fact, Python is used by beginners writing their first program and by professionals building real-world applications such as websites, business tools, data analysis systems, and automation scripts. The same simple language you learn as a beginner is powerful enough to be used by companies like Google, Netflix, and Instagram.

Chapter 5
Repeating Tasks Using Loops
Do This 5 Times!
1 2 3 4 5...
1
2
3
4
Invoce 1
Invoice 2
Invoice 3
for Loop
Repeat 5 Times
while Loop
Keep Repeating
for i in rang(5):
Repeat 5 Times
while Loop:
Ikeep condition:
for i in range(5):
while condition:

5.1 Why Repetition Needs Logic

So far, you have learned:

- How to **store data using variables**
- How to **make decisions using if–else**

But imagine this situation:

You have marks of **50 students**, and you want to:

- Check if each student passed or failed
- Print their result

Without loops, you would have to write the same if–else logic **50 times**.

That would be:

- Boring
- Error-prone
- Impossible to manage

This is where **loops** come in.

A **loop** allows Python to:

Repeat the *same logic* for *multiple values* automatically.

Loops do not introduce new thinking.

They simply **repeat what you already know** (variables + decisions).

Let us take a daily life example of class attendance. A teacher does not ask attendance for **one student only**.

They repeat the same question:

"Are you present?"

For **every student** in the class.

This repetition is exactly what loops handle.

Without a Loop (Bad Way)

print("Student 1 present")
print("Student 2 present")
print("Student 3 present")

This works only for **very small cases.**

With a Loop (Correct Way)

```
for student in range(1, 4):
    print("Student", student, "present")
```

Here:

- student is a **variable**
- range(1, 4) tells Python **how many times** to repeat
- The print statement runs **multiple times automatically**

☞ This shows how **variables + loops** work together.

The **for** Loop – Repeating with a Known Count

The for loop is used when:

You already know **how many times** a task must repeat.

Example: Printing Numbers (Revisiting Variables)

```
for number in range(1, 6):
    print(number)
```

Python does this internally:

- Stores number = 1, prints it
- Then number = 2, prints it
- Continues until 5

You already understand variables—a loop just **changes the variable value automatically**.

"The Quiet Builder"

EXERCISE: BUILDING SOMETHING PIECE BY PIECE

Many useful outputs are not written at once—they are assembled gradually.

YOUR TASK

Create a list containing the following words:

- PY
- LOGIC
- FLOW
- DATA
- REAL

Using a loop, combine these words into **one single string**, separated by hyphens.

Let's take the school example forward. Can we checking Pass/Fail for Multiple Students?

Let's connect this to **Chapter 4 (if–else)**.

```
marks = [45, 32, 67, 80]

for score in marks:
    if score >= 40:
        print("Pass")
    else:
        print("Fail")
```

What is happening:

- marks is a **list** (from Chapter 3 – advanced preview)
- score stores one value at a time
- The **same if–else logic** runs for each student

☞ This is **real programming**—combining concepts.

The while Loop – Repeating Until a Condition Changes

The while loop is used when:

You do **not know** how many times repetition is needed.

Instead, repetition depends on a **condition.**

Real-Life Example: Password Entry

You don't know how many times a user will type the wrong password. So you keep asking **until the condition is satisfied.**

```
password = ""
while password != "python":
    password = input("Enter password: ")
print("Access Granted")
```

Let's connect this to earlier chapters:

- password → variable
- != → comparison operator (decision)
- while → repeats the decision

☞ This is **decision-making inside repetition.**

Important Warning: Infinite Loops

If the condition **never becomes false**, the loop never ends.

```
while True:
    print("Hello")
```

This is called an **infinite loop** and must be avoided.

5.2 Real-World Applications Using Loops + Decisions

Let's see how everything fits together in real systems.

Banking System: Checking Multiple Transactions

```
transactions = [2000, 500, 3000]
balance = 2500
for amount in transactions:
    if balance >= amount:
        print("Transaction Approved")
    else:
        print("Insufficient Balance")
```

Uses:

- Variables (balance, amount)
- Loop (for)
- Decision (if–else)

Let's see what is happening here.

```
transactions = [2000, 500, 3000]
```

This is a **list** storing multiple withdrawal amounts. Each value represents one transaction request.

```
balance = 2500
```

- This variable stores the current bank balance.

for amount in transactions:

- Python picks **one transaction amount at a time** from the list.
- The variable amount changes automatically in each loop cycle.

if balance >= amount:

- Python compares the balance with the current transaction amount.
- This uses **decision-making logic**

print("Transaction Approved")

Runs if there is enough balance.

else: print("Insufficient Balance")

Runs if balance is not enough. This is exactly how **ATM and banking software** works internally.

HR System: Checking Training Requirement

```
experience_years = [0.5, 3, 1.2]
for exp in experience_years:
    if exp < 2:
        print("Training Required")
    else:
        print("No Training Needed")
```

So, how is it working? Could you figure out what it is doing?

experience_years = [0.5, 3, 1.2]

- A list containing experience (in years) of multiple employees.

for exp in experience_years:

- Python checks **each employee one by one**.
- exp stores one employee's experience at a time.

if exp < 2:

- Company rule: employees with less than 2 years' experience need training.

```
print("Training Required")
```

Runs for junior employees.

```
print("No Training Needed")
```

Runs for experienced employees.

E-Commerce: Processing Cart Items

```
cart = [500, 1200, 300]
total = 0
for price in cart:
    total = total + price
print("Total Bill:", total)
```

This example shows:

- Variable updating inside a loop
- Real shopping logic

Let's drill down:

```
cart = [500, 1200, 300]
```

- A list storing prices of items in the shopping cart.

```
total = 0
```

- Variable to store the final bill amount.
- Starts from zero.

for price in cart:

- Python picks each item price one by one.

total = total + price

- Adds the current item price to the running total.
- This line runs multiple times, once for each item.

print("Total Bill:", total)

- Shows the final bill after all items are added.

All three examples show the **same pattern**:

1. Store data using variables
2. Repeat using loops
3. Decide using if–else
4. Produce output

This is the foundation of real software development.

5.3 Case Study 1

Building a Student Result Processing System

Background

Imagine you are working as a **junior Python intern** in an educational technology (EdTech) company. The company runs **online tests for schools**, and they need a **basic system** that can:

- Store marks of students
- Decide whether each student has **passed or failed**
- Display results clearly

Since this is a **small pilot project**, you are asked to build a **mini version** of the system using only basic Python concepts.

You are **not expected to build a full app**—only the **logic**.

What You Have Learned So Far

You already know how to:

- Store values using **variables**
- Store multiple values using **lists**
- Make decisions using **if–else**
- Repeat tasks using **loops**

This case study uses **only these concepts.**

Problem Statement

Create a Python program that:

- Stores marks of multiple students
- Checks each student's marks
- Prints whether the student has **Passed** or **Failed**

Rules

- Passing marks = **40**
- Marks are out of **100**
- Results should be printed one by one

Input Data (Given)

Use the following marks list:

marks = [78, 35, 50, 20, 90]

Each value represents the marks of one student.

Expected Output (Example)

Student 1: Pass

Student 2: Fail

Student 3: Pass

Student 4: Fail

Student 5: Pass

Your Tasks (Step-by-Step)

Task 1

Store the marks in a variable.

Task 2

Use a **loop** to go through each student's marks.

Task 3

Use **if–else** to decide:

- Pass → marks ≥ 40
- Fail → marks < 40

Task 4

Print the result in a readable format.

Bonus Challenge (Optional, For Curious Learners)

Try to:

- Count how many students passed
- Count how many students failed

(Hint: use variables like pass_count and fail_count)

Hands-On Practice: Running This in Jupyter Notebook

You are encouraged to **test this case study in Jupyter Notebook**, just like real developers do. Below is **complete beginner guidance**.

What Is Jupyter Notebook? Jupyter Notebook is a tool that allows you to:

- Write Python code
- Run it line by line
- See output instantly
- Experiment safely

It is widely used by:

- Students
- Data scientists
- Python learners

How to Open Jupyter Notebook

Option 1: Using Anaconda (Recommended for Beginners)

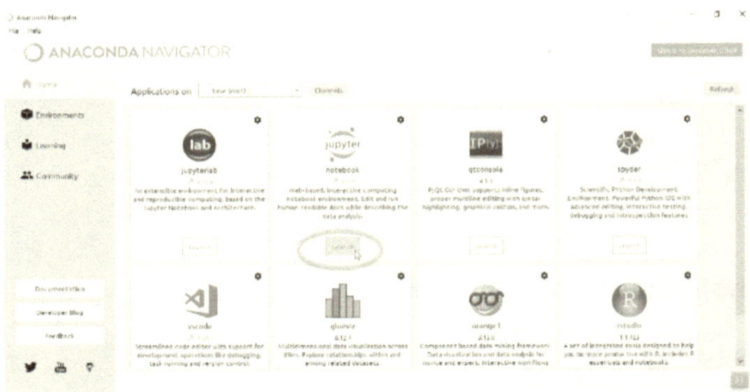

- Download **Anaconda** from the official website
- Install it (Next → Next → Finish is fine)
- Open **Anaconda Navigator**
- Click **Launch** under *Jupyter Notebook*
- Your browser will open automatically

Option 2: If Jupyter Is Already Installed

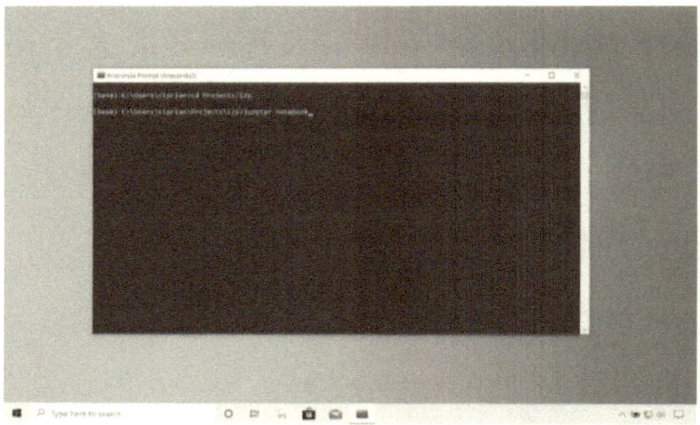

- Open **Command Prompt** (Windows) or **Terminal** (Mac/Linux)
- Type:
- jupyter notebook
- Press Enter

Creating a New Notebook

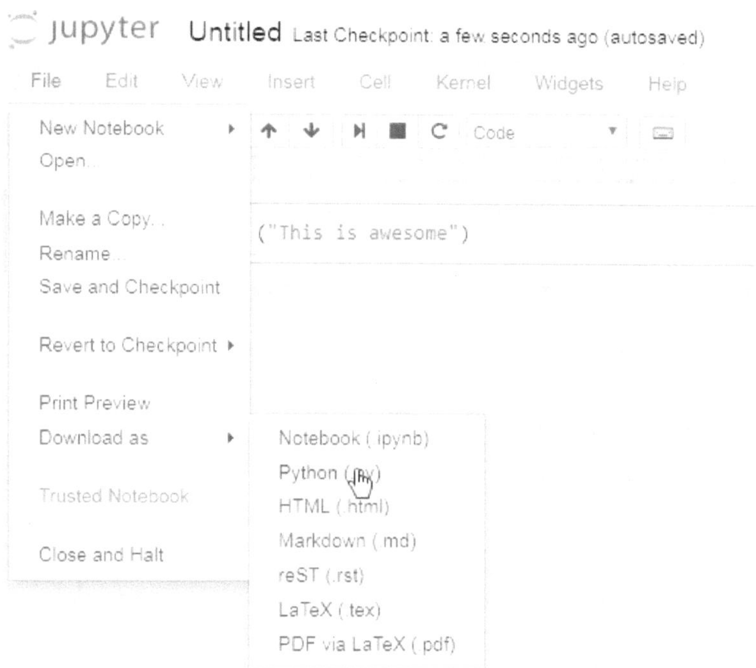

- In Jupyter, click **New** (top-right corner)
- Select **Python 3**
- A new notebook opens

How to Write and Run Code in Jupyter

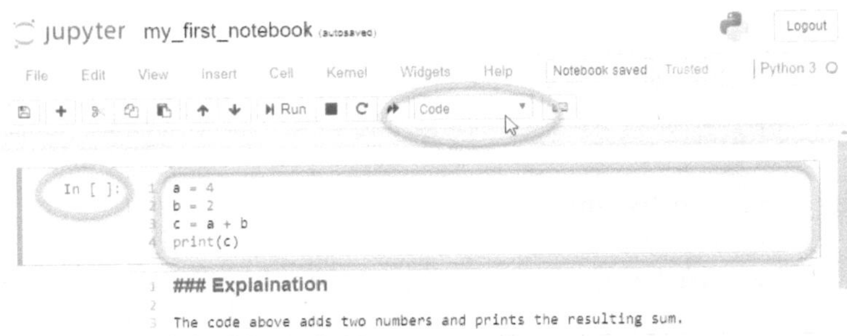

- Type Python code inside a cell
- Press **Shift + Enter** to run the cell
- Output appears below the cell

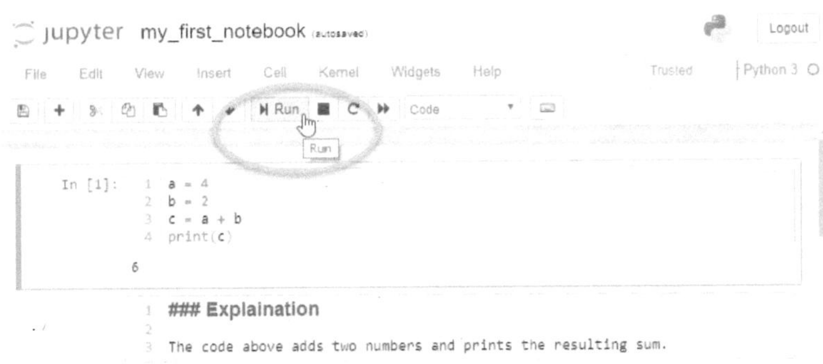

You can run the same code multiple times and change values.

5.4 Case Study 2

Building a Student Education System

Background (Real-World Context)

Imagine you are working as a **junior Python intern** in an educational technology (EdTech) company.

The company runs **online tests for schools**, and they need a **basic system** that can:

- Store marks of students
- Decide whether each student has **passed or failed**
- Display results clearly

Since this is a **small pilot project**, you are asked to build a **mini version** of the system using only basic Python concepts.

You are **not expected to build a full app**—only the **logic**.

What You Have Learned So Far

You already know how to:

- Store values using **variables**
- Store multiple values using **lists**
- Make decisions using **if–else**
- Repeat tasks using **loops**

This case study uses **only these concepts.**

Problem Statement

Create a Python program that:

- Stores marks of multiple students
- Checks each student's marks
- Prints whether the student has **Passed** or **Failed**

Rules

- Passing marks = **40**
- Marks are out of **100**
- Results should be printed one by one

Input Data (Given)

Use the following marks list:

marks = [78, 35, 50, 20, 90]

Each value represents the marks of one student.

Expected Output (Example)

Student 1: Pass

Student 2: Fail

Student 3: Pass

Student 4: Fail

Student 5: Pass

Your Tasks (Step-by-Step)

Task 1: Store the marks in a variable.

Task 2: Use a **loop** to go through each student's marks.

Task 3: Use **if–else** to decide:

- Pass → marks ≥ 40
- Fail → marks < 40

Task 4: Print the result in a readable format.

Bonus Challenge (Optional, For Curious Learners)

Try to:

- Count how many students passed
- Count how many students failed

(Hint: use variables like pass_count and fail_count)

Hands-On Practice: Running This in Jupyter Notebook

You are encouraged to **test this case study in Jupyter Notebook**, just like real developers do.

Below is **complete beginner guidance.**

How to Test the Case Study

1. Copy the given marks list into a cell
2. Write your logic below it
3. Run the cell
4. Observe output
5. Modify marks and test again

👉 **This experimentation is how programmers learn.**

Important Learning Advice

Do not try to memorize the solution.

Try to **understand the flow**:

- Data → Loop → Decision → Output

Where Is the Answer?

📌 **Important Note for Learners**

The complete solution for this case study is provided at the **end of the book**, along with answers to all chapter assessments and exercises.

Try solving it **on your own first** before checking the answer.

Why these Case Studies Matter

By completing this case study, you have:

- Built a **real-world feature**
- Combined multiple Python concepts
- Written logic similar to real applications
- Used a professional tool (Jupyter Notebook)

You are no longer just *learning Python* —you are **thinking like a programmer**.

Learning to Debug: Understanding Errors in Python

Why Errors Are Not a Bad Thing

When beginners see an error, they often think:

"I am bad at programming."

This is **not true**.

In reality:

- Errors mean Python is **talking back to you**
- Even professional programmers get errors **every day**
- Debugging is a **skill**, not a weakness

💡 **Important Truth:**

If you are not getting errors, you are not learning enough.

What Is Debugging?

Debugging means:

- Finding mistakes in your code
- Understanding why they happened
- Fixing them step by step

Python errors are actually **helpful messages** that explain:

- What went wrong
- Where it went wrong

Common Errors Beginners Face (And Why They Happen)

Let's look at **real errors** learners will face while solving your case studies.

1. Syntax Error – When Python Doesn't Understand Your Code

Example Error

```
if marks >= 40
    print("Pass")
```

What Python Shows

```
In [2]:  import sys
         sys.version

Out[2]: '2.7.13 |Anaconda custom (64-bit)| (default, Dec 19 2016, 13:29:36) [MSC v.1500 64 bit (AMD64)]'

In [1]:  print 'hello'

           File "<ipython-input-1-bfbe230352b8>", line 1
             print 'hello'
                         ^
         SyntaxError: invalid syntax
```

```
Python Shell
File  Edit  Shell  Debug  Options  Windows  Help
Python 3.1.1 (r311:74483, Aug 17 2009, 17:02:12) [MSC v.1500 32 bit (Intel)] on
win32
Type "copyright", "credits" or "license()" for more information.
>>> sam_age = 15
>>> jim_age = 12
>>> if jim_age > sam_age:
        print("sam is older")
        else:

SyntaxError: invalid syntax (<pyshell#4>, line 3)
>>> |
```

```
        self-explanatory.  If ``test_data`` is provided then the
        network will be evaluated against the test data after each
        epoch, and partial progress printed out.  This is useful for
        tracking progress, but slows things down substantially."""
        if test_data: n_test = len(test_data)
        n = len(training_data)
        for j in xrange(epochs):
            random.shuffle(training_data)
            mini_batches = [
                training_data[k:k+mini_batch_size]
                for k in xrange(0, n, mini_batch_size)]
            for mini_batch in mini_batches:
                self.update_mini_batch(mini_batch, eta)
            if test_data:
                print "Epoch {0}: {1} / {2}".format(j, self.evaluate(test_data), n_test)
            else:
                print "Epoch {0} complete".format(j)

  File "<ipython-input-3-6bc665231d08>", line 21
    print "Epoch {0}: {1} / {2}".format(j, self.evaluate(test_data), n_test)

SyntaxError: invalid syntax
```

Why This Happens

- Python expected a : after the if condition
- Python is very strict about syntax

How to Fix It

if marks >= 40:
    print("Pass")

☞ Learning Point:

Syntax errors happen when Python cannot *read* your instructions.

2. Indentation Error – Very Common in if–else and Loops

Example Error

if marks >= 40:
print("Pass")

What Python Shows

```
In [9]: class Animal():

    Input In [9]
      class Animal():
                     ^
    IndentationError: expected an indented block
```

```
def myfunc(a,b):
    if a%2==0 and b%2==0:
        if a>b:
            return b
        else:
            return a
    if a%2!=0 or b%2!=0:
         if a>b:
            return a
        else:
            return b

  File "<tokenize>", line 10
    else:
    ^
IndentationError: unindent does not match any outer indentation level
```

Why This Happens

- Python uses **spaces** to understand blocks
- print() must be indented under it

Correct Code

if marks >= 40:
    print("Pass")

☞ Learning Point:

Indentation tells Python **what belongs inside what.**

3. Name Error – Using a Variable That Does Not Exist

Example Error

print(total)

(But total was never created.)

What Python Shows

Why This Happens

- Python cannot find a variable named total
- Maybe you misspelled it or forgot to create it

Fix

```
total = 0
print(total)
```

☞ **Learning Point:**

Python does not guess variable names.

4. Logical Error – The Most Dangerous Error

This is when:

- Python runs successfully
- But the output is **wrong**

Example

```
total = 0
cart = [500, 1200, 300]

for price in cart:
    total = price

print(total)
```

Output

300

Why This Is Wrong

- The total should be 2000
- But the code **replaces** total instead of adding

Correct Code

```
for price in cart:
    total = total + price
```

☞ Learning Point:

No error message ≠ correct logic.

How to Debug Step by Step

Rule 1: Read the Error Message Slowly

- Look at the **last line**
- It usually tells you the problem

Rule 2: Check These First

- Missing :
- Wrong indentation
- Misspelled variable names

Rule 3: Print Values

Use print() to see what's happening.

```
print(price)
print(total)
```

This is called **manual debugging**—and it's powerful.

Debugging in Jupyter Notebook

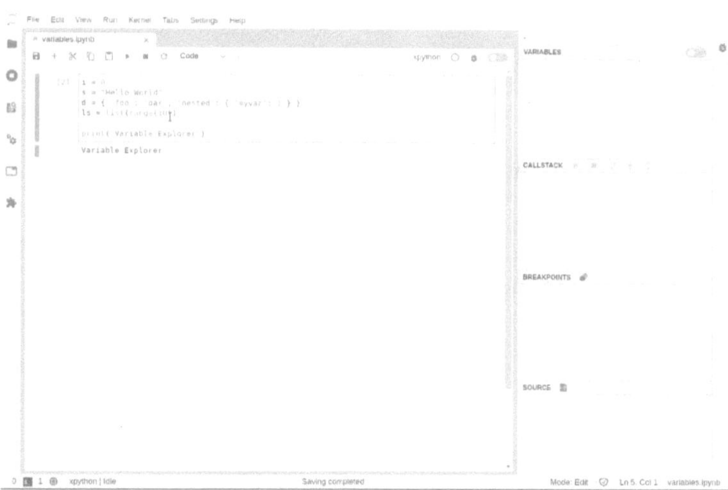

In Jupyter:

- You can run code **line by line**
- Fix mistakes instantly
- Re-run without restarting everything

🔍 **Golden Rules**

- Errors are teachers, not enemies
- Read error messages—don't panic
- Fix one error at a time
- Use print() to understand flow
- Everyone struggles—even experts

How Debugging Fits into Everything You've Learned

By now, you can:

- Store data → variables
- Decide → if–else
- Repeat → loops
- Fix mistakes → debugging

☞ This is **real programming**.

Key Takeaways

- Loops are used to **repeat tasks automatically**.
- Repetition avoids writing the same code again and again.
- Python mainly uses two loops:
  - for loop → when the number of repetitions is known
  - while loop → when repetition depends on a condition
- Loops work closely with:
  - **Variables** (to store and update values)
  - **if–else** (to make decisions during repetition)
- In a for loop, the loop variable changes automatically.
- In a while loop, the condition must eventually become false.
- An **infinite loop** happens when a loop never stops.
- Most real-world programs use **loops + decisions together**.
- Banking systems, HR systems, schools, and e-commerce apps all rely on loops.
- Understanding loops means you can now process **multiple pieces of data**, not just one.

Let's check your understanding

5A. Multiple Choice Questions

1. What is the main purpose of a loop in Python?

   a) To store data

   b) To make decisions

   c) To repeat tasks

   d) To end a program

2. Which loop is best used when you know how many times a task must repeat?

   a) while

   b) if

   c) for

   d) else

3. Which loop continues running as long as a condition is true?

   a) for

   b) while

   c) print

   d) range

4. What does range(1, 6) generate?

   a) Numbers from 1 to 6

   b) Numbers from 0 to 5

   c) Numbers from 1 to 5

   d) Infinite numbers

5. What is an infinite loop?

   a) A loop that runs very fast

   b) A loop that never ends

   c) A loop that runs once

   d) A loop with syntax error

5B. Short Answer Questions

6. Explain loops using a daily-life example.
7. What is the difference between a for loop and a while loop?
8. Why should infinite loops be avoided?

5C. Practical Exercises

9. Write a Python program to print numbers from **1 to 10** using a loop.
10. Write a Python program to:

- Store marks of students in a list
- Print **Pass** if marks ≥ 40
- Print **Fail** otherwise

11. Write a Python program to:

- Store prices of items in a cart
- Calculate and print the **total bill amount**

5D. Thinking Exercise (Conceptual)

12. In your own words, explain how **variables**, **if–else**, and **loops** work together in a real application (for example: school, banking, or shopping).

Reminder for Learners

- If loops feel confusing at first, practice small examples.
- Try changing values and re-running code in Jupyter Notebook.
- Mastery comes from practice, not memorization.

Chapter 6

How Python Learns to Make Decisions

Because real life doesn't run in straight lines.

6.1 How Python Learns to Make Decisions

Let's pause for a moment. Up to now, everything you've written in Python has followed a simple rule:

Python does exactly what you tell it to do—line by line.

No questions.

No choices.

No thinking.

And that's okay… but it's also limiting. Because real life doesn't work in straight lines.

Sometimes it rains.

Sometimes it doesn't.

Sometimes a user enters the correct password.

Sometimes they don't.

If Python couldn't handle these differences, it would be useless in the real world. That's why this chapter is important. This is the chapter where Python stops being a calculator and starts behaving like a **decision-maker**.

Before we write even one line of code, let's clear something up. Programming is **not** about memorizing keywords like if, else, or elif. Programming is about answering questions like:

- *What should happen if this is true?*
- *What should happen if it's not?*
- *What are all the possible situations?*

You already do this every day—without realizing it. Let's look at some examples from your own life:

- **If** your phone battery is low → you charge it
- **If** traffic is heavy → you leave early

- **If** today is Sunday → you relax
- **Else** → you go to work

You don't call this "logic." You just call it **thinking**. Python works the same way. The only difference is:

☞ You must explain your thinking **very clearly** to Python.

Teaching Python to Ask a Question:

The if statement is how Python asks a question. Here's a very simple example:

```
age = 18
if age >= 18:
    print("You are allowed to vote")
```

Now don't rush. Let's read this **slowly**, like a human sentence:

"If age is greater than or equal to 18, then print this message."

That's it. There is nothing hidden here. No trick. No complexity. Python checks the condition:

- If it's **True**, the message appears
- If it's **False**, Python silently moves on

Why Python Needs Indentation

Python uses indentation (spaces) to understand which lines belong together.

```
if age >= 18:
    print("Allowed")
    print("Welcome")
```

Those spaces before print are not decoration. They are meaning. They tell Python:

"These lines belong to the if condition."

If you remove the indentation, Python gets confused—and so will you.

Think of indentation as:

📦 putting related ideas into the same box.

Once this clicks, Python becomes much easier than languages full of symbols.

What If the Answer Is "No"? Meet else

Real life always has alternatives. So Python gives you else.

```
age = 15


if age >= 18:
    print("You can vote")
else:
    print("You are not eligible")
```

Here's something important and comforting:

👉 **Python will never run both blocks.**

Only one path will execute.

That predictability is what makes programs reliable.

Let's be honest—most situations are not black and white. Life Rarely Has Just Two Outcomes. Marks. Salaries. Weather. Experience levels. That's where elif comes in.

```
marks = 82


if marks >= 90:
    print("Excellent")
elif marks >= 75:
    print("Very good")
```

```
elif marks >= 60:
    print("Good")
else:
    print("Needs improvement")
```

How Python reads this:

- Start from the top
- Check each condition
- Stop at the **first true one**

This is why **order matters**. Python doesn't look ahead. It trusts the order you give it.

How Python Compares Things

To make decisions, Python needs comparison tools. Here are the ones you'll use all the time:

Operator	Meaning
==	equal
!=	not equal
>	greater than
<	less than
>=	greater than or equal
<=	less than or equal

⚠ A very common beginner mistake:

```
if age = 18:   # ✗ wrong
```

Why?

Because = **assigns** a value.

== **compares** values.

This mistake is normal. Everyone makes it. What matters is catching it early—which you just did.

Real decisions often depend on **multiple factors.**

Example:

- User must be above 18
- AND must have an ID

```
age = 22
has_id = True
if age >= 18 and has_id:
    print("Entry allowed")
```

Think in plain English:

- and → everything must be true
- or → at least one must be true
- not → reverse the condition

This is how Python mirrors real thinking. At this point, a beginner often wonders:

"Okay... this makes sense in examples. But where does this really get used?"

The answer is simple—**everywhere.**

If a program ever needs to *decide* something, conditional logic is involved. Let's walk through some real situations you already interact with daily. Let's connect this to the real world systems .

Login systems

Every time you log into:

- Gmail
- Instagram

- Your bank app
- Your company portal

A decision is being made.

Not once.

But multiple times.

Let's start small.

```
username = input("Enter username: ")
password = input("Enter password: ")

if username == "admin" and password == "python123":
    print("Login successful")
else:
    print("Invalid credentials")
```

What's really happening here?

The program is asking:

- Did the user enter the **correct username**?
- Did they enter the **correct password**?

Only if **both** answers are "yes" does access get granted.

In real applications:

- Passwords are encrypted
- Data comes from databases
- Security is much stronger

But at the core, the thinking is still:

If credentials match → allow access

Else → deny access

Every secure system starts with this logic. Every one of these depends on **conditional logic**. Without if, Python cannot interact with reality.

Banking Systems: "Can This Transaction Happen?"

When you withdraw money from an ATM or app, the system doesn't just obey you blindly. It checks conditions. Think about it:

- Do you have enough balance?
- Is the amount valid?
- Has your daily limit been exceeded?

Here's a simplified version:

```
balance = 5000

withdraw_amount = int(input("Enter amount to withdraw: "))

if withdraw_amount <= balance:
    balance = balance - withdraw_amount
    print("Transaction successful")
    print("Remaining balance:", balance)
else:
    print("Insufficient balance")
```

This tiny program captures a **real financial rule**: Money cannot be withdrawn if it doesn't exist.

In real banks, Python (or similar logic) runs:

- Fraud checks
- Limit checks
- Account status checks

But they all depend on **conditional decisions**.

Websites: "What Should This User See?"

Ever noticed how:

- Logged-in users see dashboards
- Logged-out users see login pages
- Admins see extra buttons?

That's not magic. That's if–else.

```
is_logged_in = False

if is_logged_in:
    print("Welcome to your dashboard")
else:
    print("Please log in to continue")
```

Behind every website:

- Python checks your session
- Decides what page to show
- Decides what actions are allowed

Even something as small as:

"Show Logout button or Login button?"

...is controlled by conditional logic.

Games: "What Happens Next?"

Games are full of decisions—constantly.

- Did the player lose all health?
- Did they collect enough points?
- Did time run out?

```
health = 0

if health <= 0:
    print("Game Over")
else:
    print("Keep playing")
```

In real games, this logic controls:

- Lives
- Levels
- Power-ups
- Enemy behavior

Games feel exciting because they **react** to your actions.

And reaction = decisions.

Age-Based Rules: Tickets, Content, Access

You've seen this everywhere:

- Movie ratings
- Alcohol purchase
- Online content warnings

```
age = int(input("Enter your age: "))

if age < 13:
    print("Child content")
elif age < 18:
    print("Teen content")
else:
    print("Adult content")
```

This is Python enforcing **rules**, just like society does.

E-commerce: "Can You Buy This?"

When you shop online, the system checks:

- Is the item in stock?
- Is payment successful?
- Is delivery available to your location?

Example:

```
in_stock = True
payment_done = True

if in_stock and payment_done:
    print("Order confirmed")
else:
    print("Order failed")
```

Without these checks, online shopping would be chaos.

A Very Important Realization (Pause Here)

Notice something?

All these examples:

- Look different
- Belong to different industries
- Feel complex in real life

But underneath, they all use the **same thinking pattern**:

If this condition is true → do this

Else → do something else

Once you master this pattern,

you are no longer "learning Python",

you are **learning how software thinks.**

Why Beginners Often Struggle Here (And Why It's Normal)

This chapter feels harder because:

- Python is no longer just executing
- It's evaluating situations
- It's choosing paths

Your brain is shifting from:

"What do I type?"

to:

"What should happen?"

That shift takes time—and that's okay.

One Last Thought Before You Move On

Every advanced Python feature you'll learn later—loops, functions, databases, web apps, AI. **All of them depend on conditional logic.** This chapter is not "just another topic." It is **a foundation chapter**. Take your time with it. Play with examples. Change values and observe results. That's how real understanding forms.

6.2 How Python Decisions Show Up in Everyday Life

Let's step away from code for a moment and talk about **people**. Because Python is not really about machines, it's about solving **human problems.**

Riya and the Login Screen

Riya is a college student. Every morning, the first thing she does is open her email. One day, she types her password too fast. Instead of entering her inbox, she sees:

❌ *Incorrect password. Please try again.*

What just happened?

The system didn't get angry. It didn't crash. It simply **checked a condition**. Behind the scenes, the program asked:

Does the entered password match the stored one?

If yes → allow access

If no → show an error

That's an if–else decision.

```
if entered_password == stored_password:
    allow_access
else:
    deny_access
```

Every secure system you trust starts with this simple idea.

Aman at the ATM

Aman goes to an ATM late at night.

He tries to withdraw ₹10,000.

But his account balance is only ₹7,000. The machine doesn't argue.

It doesn't ask him to try harder. It simply says:

✕ *Insufficient balance.*

Why? Because before giving money, the ATM checks:

Is the withdrawal amount ≤ balance?

```
if withdraw_amount <= balance:
    dispense_cash
else:
    show_error
```

This one condition protects:

- The bank
- The system
- Aman himself

That's the power of decisions in code.

Neha Browsing a Website

Neha visits an online learning platform.

- When she's logged in → she sees her courses
- When she's logged out → she sees the login page

Same website. Same URL. Different experience. Why?

Because the website asks:

Is this user logged in?

```
if is_logged_in:
    show_dashboard
else:
    show_login_page
```

This decision is made **every time a page loads**. Without it, websites wouldn't feel personal.

Arjun Playing a Game

Arjun is playing a game after a long day. His character gets hit again… and again… and again. Suddenly:

💀 *Game Over*

Why didn't the game continue?

Because the game constantly checks:

Is the player's health zero?

```
if health <= 0:
    end_game
else:
    continue_game
```

Games feel exciting because they **respond.** And response comes from conditional logic.

Online Shopping Checkout

You click **"Buy Now."** But before the order is confirmed, the system checks:

- Is the item in stock?
- Is payment successful?
- Is delivery available?

```
if in_stock and payment_successful:
    confirm_order
else:
    cancel_order
```

These checks protect you from:

- Paying for unavailable items
- Failed transactions
- Broken promises

Every story you just read:

- Uses different words
- Happens in different industries
- Feels complex in real life

But inside the computer…

☞ **It's always the same thinking pattern.**

If this is true → do this

Else → do something else

Once this clicks, programming stops feeling mysterious.

Learn by Thinking, Not Memorizing

⚠ **Important rule:**

Don't rush. Even writing *half* the logic is progress.

Let's try some exercises.

Exercise 1: Login Attempt

Scenario:

Ask the user for a password. If it matches "python", print "Access granted." Otherwise, print "Access denied."

💡 Think first:

- What is the condition?
- What happens if it's true?
- What happens if it's false?

Write your code here:

Exercise 2: ATM Withdrawal

Scenario:

- Set balance = 3000
- Ask user for withdrawal amount

If amount is less than or equal to balance:

- Deduct it
- Print remaining balance

Else:

- Print "Insufficient balance"

Write your code here:

Exercise 3: Website Access

Scenario:

Create a variable is_logged_in.

- If true → print "Welcome back!"
- Else → print "Please log in."

Try changing the value and run the program again.

Write your code here:

Exercise 4: Game Health Check

Scenario:

Create a variable health.

- If health is 0 or less → print "Game Over"
- Else → print "Keep playing"

Write your code here:

Exercise 5: Age-Based Access

Scenario:

Ask user for age.

- Below 13 → "Child access"
- 13 to 17 → "Teen access"
- 18 and above → "Adult access"

Write your code here:

If your brain feels tired right now—that's good. This chapter isn't about typing fast. It's about **thinking clearly**. You didn't just learn Python syntax. You learned how software decides. And that skill stays with you forever.

Before You Move On

Ask yourself:

- Can I explain an if–else without code?
- Can I describe the decision in words?
- Can I predict what a program will do before running it?

If yes—you're ready for the next chapter.

Key Takeaways

- Python makes decisions using **conditions**
- if lets Python ask a question
- else tells Python what to do when the answer is "no"
- elif helps when there are **multiple possibilities**
- Indentation shows Python *what belongs together*
- and, or, and not help combine real-life conditions
- Every login, game, website, and banking app depends on this logic
- You now think less like a user and more like a **programmer**

Let's check your understanding

6A. Concept Check (Answer in Words)

- What does an if statement do in your own words?
- Why does Python care so much about indentation?
- What happens if **multiple elif conditions are true**?
- What is the difference between = and ==?
- When would you use and instead of or?

If you can explain these without code—you understand them.

6B. Code Thinking (No Pressure)

Look at this code:

```
age = 16

if age >= 18:
    print("Adult")
else:
    print("Minor")
```

- What will be printed?
- Why?

Now change age to 21 in your head.

- What changes?
- Why?

☞ If you can predict outcomes without running code,

you are **thinking like a programmer**.

6C. Try This (Optional but Powerful)

Write *any one* of the following without looking back:

- A login check
- A game over condition
- An ATM withdrawal check
- An age-based decision

Even half-correct logic counts.

🌱 A Gentle Closing Note to the Learner

If this chapter felt heavier than earlier ones—that's normal.

You didn't just learn syntax.

You learned **decision-making logic**, and that's a big step.

From here on:

- Code starts to feel *alive*
- Programs start to *react*
- Python starts to feel *useful*

You've crossed an invisible but important line.

6D. The Quiz

1. What is the main purpose of an if statement in Python?

    a) To repeat tasks

    b) To store values

    c) To make decisions

    d) To display output

2. Which keyword is used when the condition in if is false?

   a) elif

   b) else

   c) while

   d) break

3. What does the symbol == mean in Python?

   a) Assignment

   b) Comparison

   c) Looping

   d) Printing

4. Which of the following operators is used to check multiple conditions together?

   a) =

   b) and

   c) print

   d) input

5. What will Python do if multiple elif conditions are true?

   a) Run all of them

   b) Run the last one

   c) Run the first true one

   d) Throw an error

6E. Short Answer Questions

6. Explain decision-making in Python using a real-life example (such as login, ATM, or school grading).

7. Why is indentation important in Python while using if–else statements?

8. What is the difference between if and elif?

6F. Practical Exercises

9. Write a Python program to check whether a number entered by the user is positive, negative, or zero.

10. Write a Python program to:
    - Ask the user for age
    - Print **Child** if age < 13
    - Print **Teen** if age is between 13 and 17
    - Print **Adult** if age ≥ 18

11. Write a Python program to:
    - Store a variable balance = 5000
    - Ask the user for withdrawal amount
    - Print **Transaction Successful** if balance is sufficient
    - Print **Insufficient Balance** otherwise

6G. Thinking Exercise (Conceptual)

12. Think of any real-life situation (school, banking, shopping, or gaming). Explain how **conditions** help a program decide *what should happen next.*

Reminder for Learners

- If if–else feels confusing, write the logic in plain English first.
- Don't memorize syntax—understand the decision.
- Every smart program begins with clear thinking.

Chapter 7

Functions – Teaching Python to Do One Job at a Time

Because good programs are built step by step, not all at once.

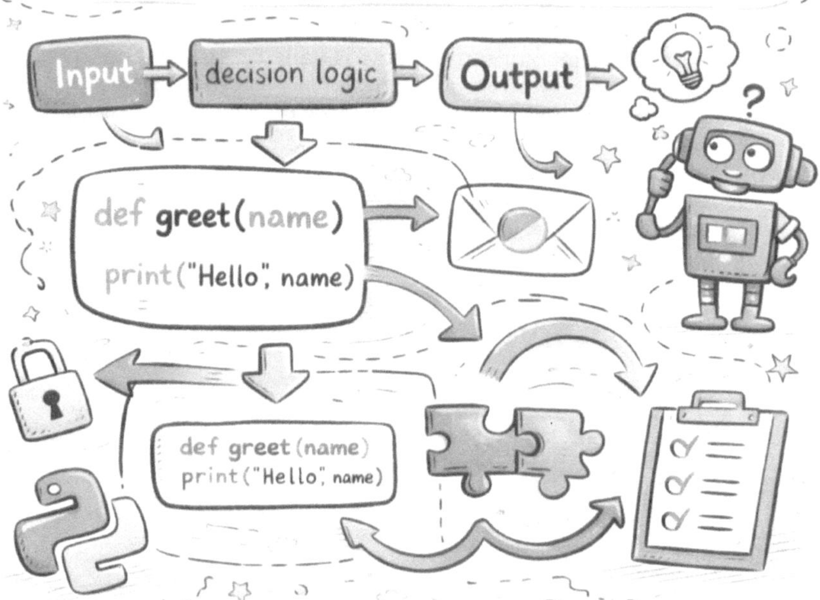

7.1 Teaching Python to do one job at a time

Let's start with a simple question.

Have you ever followed a fixed routine?

For example, sending an email:

- Open Gmail
- Click Compose
- Add the recipient
- Add CC (if needed)
- Type the subject
- Write the email
- Click Send

You don't reinvent these steps every time. You just **follow a known process**. In Python, that known process is called a **function**.

A named group of instructions that does **one specific job**.

That's the function.

- It has a **name**
- It contains **steps**
- It performs **one task**

Just like "Send email", "Calculate total", "Check result", or "Say hello"

But why Do We Even Need Functions? Before functions, imagine this: You want Python to greet a user.

You write: print("Hello John")

Now you meet another user.

You write again: print("Hello Neha")

And again. And again. And again. This becomes repetitive, messy, and hard to maintain. Functions solve this by saying:

"Write the instructions **once**,

use them **many times**."

A Function is like giving instructions, not doing them. This is **very important**, and beginners often miss it. When you define a function, Python **does not run it**. It only **learns what to do later**. Look at this:

```
def greet():
    print("Hello")
```

This tells Python:

"If someone asks you to greet, say Hello."

But Python will **not say Hello yet**. Why? Because you haven't asked it to.

To make Python run the function, you must **call it**.

```
greet()
```

Now Python says:

```
Hello
```

Think of it like this:

- def greet() → writing a recipe
- greet() → cooking the food

Writing ≠ doing.

Now let's make this more useful. Instead of greeting everyone the same way, what if we want Python to greet a **specific person**?

```
def greet(name):
    print("Hello", name)
```

Here:

- name is an **input**
- It's also called a **parameter**

Now call it:

greet("John")

The Output

```
Hello John
```

Call it again:

```
greet("Neha")
```

The Output

```
Hello Neha
```

Same function. Different data. That's power.

How is this useful in real life? Think about an ATM. The process is the same:

- Insert card
- Enter PIN
- Enter amount
- Dispense cash

But the **amount changes**. That's exactly what function inputs do. Here is a golden rule you should remember: **One function should do only one job.**

Bad example (doing too much):

```
def everything():
    check_marks()
    send_email()
    print_certificate()
```

Good example:

```
def check_marks():
    ...

def send_email():
    ...
```

Why this matters:

- Easier to understand
- Easier to fix
- Easier to reuse

This rule comes directly from real software development.

Returning a Value—Getting an Answer Back

So far, functions were **doing things**.

But sometimes, we want a function to:

- Calculate something
- Decide something
- Give us an answer

That's where return comes in. Let's say, in your school, passing marks = 40 for a student and we want Python to **decide**, not print.

```
def is_pass(marks):
    if marks >= 40:
        return True
    else:
        return False
```

This function:

- Takes marks
- Checks condition
- Returns **True or False**

Now let's use it:

```
result = is_pass(50)
print(result)
```

Output:

```
True
```

When you use return:

- The function **gives back a value**
- That value can be:
    - Stored in a variable
    - Used in another decision
    - Used in another function

Think of it like asking a question: "Did I pass?" and Python answers: "Yes (True)" or "No (False)"

7.2 How This Works in Real Applications

Let's connect this to real life. So far, you've learned that a function is:

A named group of instructions that does one job.

Now let's slow down and really understand **why this matters in the real world**. Functions are not a "Python thing". They are a **thinking pattern** used in every real application.

School System: Checking Pass or Fail

Real-Life Situation

A teacher checks whether a student has passed an exam. The rule is simple: If marks are **40 or more** → Pass. Otherwise → Fail

This decision is repeated for **every student**. Instead of rewriting the same logic again and again, we create a **function**.

> **"The Quiet Builder"**
>
> **EXERCISE: TURNING LOGIC INTO A REUSABLE TOOL**
>
> Applications are made of small ideas that can be reused again and again.
>
> **YOUR TASK**
>
> Write a Python function that:
>
> - Builds a combined code using a list of words
> - Returns the final combined string
>
> Do not print the result yet—only return it.

How a Human Thinks

"Whenever I give you marks, tell me whether the student passed."

How Python Thinks (Using a Function)

```
def is_pass(marks):
    if marks >= 40:
        return True
    else:
        return False
```

Now this function becomes a rule checker.

Using the Function

```
result = is_pass(55)

if result:
    print("Student Passed")
else:
    print("Student Failed")
```

Why This Is Powerful

- The rule is written once
- It can be reused for 1000 students
- If the passing marks change later (say to 45),

you change it in one place only

This is exactly how school software works.

Banking System: Allowing or Blocking a Withdrawal

Real-Life Situation

When you withdraw money from an ATM, the machine must decide:

- Is the balance enough?
- If yes → Allow withdrawal
- If no → Block transaction

This decision is **critical** and must be **accurate every time.**

How a Human Thinks

"Only allow withdrawal if the balance is greater than or equal to the amount."

Python Function for This Logic

```
def can_withdraw(balance, amount):
```

```
    if balance >= amount:
        return True
    else:
        return False
```

Using the Function

```
balance = 5000
amount = 2000

if can_withdraw(balance, amount):
    print("Transaction Successful")
else:
    print("Insufficient Balance")
```

Every banking app uses thousands of such small functions as:

- Banking rules must be **consistent**
- One mistake can cause **financial loss**
- Functions ensure the **same logic is applied everywhere**

Website Login System: Granting or Denying Access

Real-Life Situation

When you log into a website, the system checks: Is the password correct? This logic should not be written again and again for every page.

Human Thinking

"Whenever someone tries to log in, check if the password is correct."

Python Function

```
def check_password(input_password):
    if input_password == "python123":
```

```
        return True
    else:
        return False
```

Using the Function

```
password = input("Enter password: ")

if check_password(password):
    print("Login Successful")
else:
    print("Wrong Password")
```

In real websites, passwords are encrypted but the **decision-making pattern is the same**:

- Login logic stays in **one place**
- Security rules are easier to manage
- Code becomes **clean and readable**

HR System: Mandatory Training Decision

Real-Life Situation: A company has a policy which says 'Employees **below 25 years** must attend cultural training'. HR software must:

- Check employee age
- Decide whether training is required

Python Function

```
def is_training_required(age):
    if age < 25:
        return True
    else:
        return False
```

Using the Function

```
employee_age = 23

if is_training_required(employee_age):
    print("Training Required")
else:
    print("No Training Required")
```

Use of functions is needed here because:

- Policies change → logic updates easily
- Same rule applies to **all employees**
- HR systems remain maintainable

E-Commerce: Calculating the Total Bill

Real-Life Situation: When you shop online:

- Items are added to cart
- Total bill must be calculated

Instead of calculating manually every time, we create a function.

Python Function

```
def calculate_total(prices):
    total = 0
    for price in prices:
        total = total + price
    return total
```

Using the Function

```
cart = [200, 350, 150]

bill = calculate_total(cart)
print("Total Bill:", bill)
```

Why All These Examples Use Functions?

Real Life	Function Does
School	Checks result
Bank	Approves withdrawal
Website	Validates login
HR	Applies policy
Shopping	Calculates total

The pattern is always the same:

Give data → apply rules → return an answer

That is the true role of a function. If you understand functions, you are no longer just writing Python, copying syntax but you are **designing logic**. This is the skill that scales from small programs to large systems.

7.3 Recap

Before we jump to a real-world case study, let us divert a bit. Up to now, you've learned many powerful tools:

- Variables to store data
- if–else to make decisions
- Loops to repeat actions
- Lists to handle multiple values
- Functions to organize logic

But here's an important truth about real-world programming:

Professional developers do not start by writing code. They start by **thinking, structuring, and planning**.

This section teaches you *how* to do that.

You might ask:

"I know the syntax, but how do I build something real?"

"Where do I start?"

"How do I connect everything together?"

The answer is:

👉 **You design the flow first.**

That's exactly what professionals do.

Before a single line of Python is written, they ask:

- Who is the user?
- What is the goal?
- What decisions
- are involved?
- What can repeat?
- What should be reusable?

To answer these questions, they use **flowcharts and user flows**. You can skip this section if you already know how to create flowcharts.

What Is a Flowchart?

A **flowchart** is a visual way to show:

- Steps
- Decisions
- Repetition
- End points

It answers one simple question:

"What happens next?"

Flowcharts are **language-independent**. You can design a flowchart even if you don't know Python yet. That's why they are taught before coding in professional environments.

You do **not** need complex symbols to start. Most applications can be designed using just four shapes:

- **Start/End (Oval)**

  Marks where the program begins or finishes.

  Example:

  Start → End

- **Process (Rectangle)**

  Any action or instruction

  Examples:

  - Take input
  - Assign value
  - Calculate total
  - Call a function

- **Decision (Diamond)**

  A question with **Yes/No** outcomes

  Examples:

  - Is age ≥ 18?
  - Is password correct?
  - Is balance sufficient?
  - This maps directly to if–else.

- **Flow Arrows**
  - Show direction and sequence
  - Make logic readable

How Professionals Create User Flows

In real companies, before coding starts:

- Product managers
- Designers
- Developers

...all sit together and design **user flows.**

A **user flow** shows:

- What the user does
- What the system checks
- What happens next

It prevents confusion, missing conditions, logic errors, and rewriting code later

How *You* Can Create a User Flow?

You don't need tools or software. Follow these **5 steps**:

Step 1: Define the Goal

Ask: "What should this application finally achieve?"

Step 2: Identify Inputs

Ask: "What information does the user provide?"

Step 3: Identify Decisions

Ask: "Where does the program need to choose?"

These become **decision diamonds.**

Step 4: Identify Repetition

Ask: "What might repeat?"

These hint at **loops.**

Step 5: Identify Reusable Logic

Ask: "Which logic should be reused?"

These become **functions**.

7.4 Case Study: Student Result Management System

You are asked to design a **simple student result application** for a school. This is **not just a coding task**. You must **think like a system designer first**.

Goal of the Application

The system should:

- Accept marks of students
- Decide whether each student has passed or failed
- Display the result clearly
- Work for **multiple students**

Inputs Required

- Student name
- Marks obtained

Rules to Apply

- Passing marks = **40**
- If marks ≥ 40 → Pass
- Else → Fail

Repetition Requirement

- The system should work for **more than one student**
- It should not stop after checking just one student

Reusable Logic

- The **pass/fail check** should be written once
- It should be reused for every student

(Hint: This should be a function.)

What You Must Do (Before Writing Code)

Task 1: Write the Logic in Plain English

Example:

Start program

Take student name

Take student marks

Check if marks ≥ 40

If yes → Print Pass

Else → Print Fail

Ask if another student exists

Repeat if needed

End program

Task 2: Draw the Flowchart

You should draw a flowchart that includes:

- Start
- Input
- Decision (Pass/Fail)
- Output
- Loop (for next student)
- End

This flowchart should be drawn:

- On paper
- Or in a notebook
- Or using any simple diagram tool

The goal is **clarity**, not perfection.

Task 3: Identify Python Concepts Used

You should clearly label:

- Where variables are used
- Where if–else is used
- Where loops are needed
- Where a function fits

This builds **conceptual mastery**, not rote coding. **Do NOT jump to writing code immediately.** First:

- Think
- Draw
- Explain

Only then: Translate into Python

This is how real developers work.

Where is the Solution

☞ **The complete solution** to this case study (including: flowchart explanation, logic breakdown, Python implementation) **will be provided at the end of the book,**

Key Takeaways

- A **function** is a named group of instructions that does **one specific job**
- Defining a function (def) is **not the same** as running it
- A function runs **only when it is called**
- Functions can take **inputs (parameters)** to work with different data
- The return statement sends a result **back to the program**
- print shows output, but return is used for **logic and decisions**
- Good programs use **many small functions**, not one large one
- Real-world systems (school, banking, websites, HR, shopping) are built using functions
- Professional developers **design logic and flow first**, before writing code
- Flowcharts help visualize: steps

  Decisions, repetition, and end points

Let's check your understanding

7A. Multiple Choice Questions

1. What is the main purpose of a function in Python?

   a) To repeat tasks

   b) To store data

   c) To organize instructions for one job

   d) To stop a program

2. Which keyword is used to define a function in Python?

   a) function

   b) define

   c) def

   d) return

3. What happens when a function is defined but not called?

   a) It runs automatically

   b) It causes an error

   c) Python remembers it but does not execute it

   d) The program stops

4. What does the return statement do?

   a) Prints output

   b) Ends the program

   c) Sends a value back to the caller

   d) Repeats the function

5. Why should one function ideally perform only one task?

   a) To make programs longer

   b) To make code faster

   c) To keep code clean and reusable

   d) Because Python requires it

7B. Short Answer Questions

6. Explain what a function is using a real-life example (such as ATM, school, or email).
7. What is the difference between print and return in a function?
8. Why is it important to *call* a function after defining it?

7C. Practical Thinking Exercises

9. Write a function that takes **marks** as input and returns **True** if the student passes (marks ≥ 40), otherwise returns **False.**
10. Write a function that:

- Takes **balance** and **withdrawal amount**
- Returns whether withdrawal is allowed or not

(Do not print inside the function.)

7D. Flowchart & Application Design Exercise (Very Important)

11. You are asked to design a **Student Result Management System.**

Before writing code, do the following:

a) Write the program logic in plain English

- What happens first?
- What inputs are required?
- Where are decisions made?
- What repeats?

b) Draw a flowchart that includes:

- Start and End
- Input steps
- Decision (Pass/Fail)
- Loop for multiple students

c) Identify:

- Which part should be a function
- Which part needs if–else
- Which part needs a loop

⚠ **Do not write code yet.**

Focus on **thinking and flow design**.

7E. Case Study (Capstone Thinking Task)

12. **Case Study: School Result Application**

Design an application that:

- Accepts student name and marks
- Decides pass or fail
- Repeats for multiple students
- Uses a function for decision logic

Your task is to submit:

- Flowchart
- Logic explanation
- Concept mapping (variables, decisions, loops, functions)

Chapter 8

Putting It All Together

How Real Programs Are Built

8.1 How Real Programs Are Built

Let's pause for a moment. If you're feeling slightly overwhelmed right now, that's a **good sign**. It means your brain is no longer learning isolated ideas—it's trying to **connect them**. And that's exactly what this chapter is about.

Up to now, your journey has looked like this:

- You learned how to store data
- You learned how to make decisions
- You learned how to repeat tasks
- You learned how to organize logic into functions

Individually, each of these made sense. But many learners reach this point and think:

"I know Python concepts...

but I don't know how to build something real."

That confusion is normal. Real programs are not made of **new concepts**. They are made by **connecting familiar ones correctly**. This chapter exists to help you see **the big picture**.

Before we move forward, let's quickly remind ourselves what each concept does—not how it works, but **why it exists**.

- **Variables** store information so it can be used later
- **Decisions (if–else)** allow the program to choose a path
- **Loops** let the program repeat work efficiently
- **Lists** allow us to manage multiple values together
- **Functions** organize logic into meaningful, reusable blocks

None of these work alone in real programs. They work **together**.

How Real Programs Are Actually Written

Here's an important truth that beginners are rarely told early enough: **Professional programmers do not start by writing code.**

They start by:

- Understanding the problem
- Breaking it into parts
- Designing the flow
- Deciding responsibilities
- Then writing code

When beginners jump straight into coding, they often end up with:

- Long, confusing scripts
- Repeated logic
- Hard-to-fix errors

That's not because they're bad learners—it's because they skipped the **thinking stage**.

An Integrated Example (Conceptual, Not Code)

Let's think about a simple system you already understand.

Imagine a small application that:

- Takes student marks
- Decides pass or fail
- Works for many students

At a thinking level, this system already uses:

- Variables (to store marks)
- Decisions (pass or fail)
- Loops (multiple students)
- Functions (reusable logic)

Notice something important:

☞ We haven't written any code yet.

We are still **designing**.

Designing the Flow First

This is where flowcharts come in—not as decoration, but as **clarity tools.** A flowchart answers one question: "What happens next?"

For our example, the flow might look like this (in words):

- Start
- Take student name
- Take marks
- Check if marks ≥ 40
- Show result
- Ask if another student exists
- If yes → repeat
- If no → end

This sequence is your **program**, before Python ever gets involved.

Breaking One Problem into Functions

Once the flow is clear, the next professional step is separation of responsibility. Instead of thinking:

"How do I write this program?"

Think:

"What jobs does this program do?"

For example:

- One job takes input
- One job checks pass/fail
- One job displays output

Each job becomes a **function**. This keeps your program:

- Easier to read
- Easier to debug
- Easier to expand later

Good programs grow by **adding functions**, not by stretching one giant block.

Let's understand this with a **real example**, not theory. Imagine you are building a **student result program** that:

- Takes marks
- Decides pass or fail
- Prints the result
- Repeats for multiple students

✕ The Problem: One Giant Block of Code

> **"The Quiet Builder"**
>
> **EXERCISE: LETTING USERS SPEAK TO YOUR PROGRAM**
>
> Programs become meaningful when they interact with people.
>
> **YOUR TASK**
>
> Using Jupyter Notebook:
>
> - Create three input fields for name, email, and country
> - Add a button that a user can click
> - Display the entered values when the button is clicked

A beginner might write everything in one place like this:

```
students = ["Amit", "Neha", "Ravi"]
marks = [45, 32, 78]


i = 0
while i < len(students):
    name = students[i]
    score = marks[i]
```

```
    if score >= 40:
        result = "Pass"
    else:
        result = "Fail"

    print(name, ":", result)

    i = i + 1
```

What's wrong here?

Nothing is *technically* wrong—the code works.

But as programs grow, this becomes a problem because:

- All logic is mixed together
- Decision logic is trapped inside the loop
- You can't reuse the pass/fail rule elsewhere
- Changing one rule means touching many lines

This code **does not grow well.**

✅ The Better Way: Let the Program Grow with Functions

Now let's write the **same program**, but structured properly.

Step 1: Create a Function for One Job

First, isolate the decision logic.

```
def is_pass(marks):
    if marks >= 40:
        return "Pass"
    else:
        return "Fail"
```

This function:

- Has one job
- Can be reused
- Can be changed easily later

Step 2: Use the Function Inside the Loop

Now write the main flow clearly:

```
students = ["Amit", "Neha", "Ravi"]
marks = [45, 32, 78]

i = 0
while i < len(students):
    name = students[i]
    score = marks[i]

    result = is_pass(score)
    print(name, ":", result)

    i = i + 1
```

Let's compare how both versions **grow. If the passing rule changes**

From:

marks >= 40

To:

marks >= 50

You change **only one line** inside is_pass()

The rest of the program stays untouched

If you need the same logic elsewhere

Example:

- Scholarship eligibility
- Re-exam decision
- Grade calculation later

You already have the logic ready:

```
is_pass(marks)
```

That's reuse—a professional habit.

How Professionals Think About This

Professionals don't ask: "Where do I write this code?"

They ask: "Does this logic deserve its own function?"

If the answer is yes. It becomes a function. That's how programs **scale without breaking.**

A Simple Rule to Remember

If your program feels like one long paragraph, it probably needs functions. Or even simpler:

Functions are paragraphs. Programs are essays.

Connecting This Back to the Big Idea

When we say:

"Good programs grow by adding functions, not by stretching one giant block."

We mean:

- Growth = clarity
- Clarity = separation of responsibility
- Separation = functions

This is not about writing *more* code.

It's about writing **better organized code.**

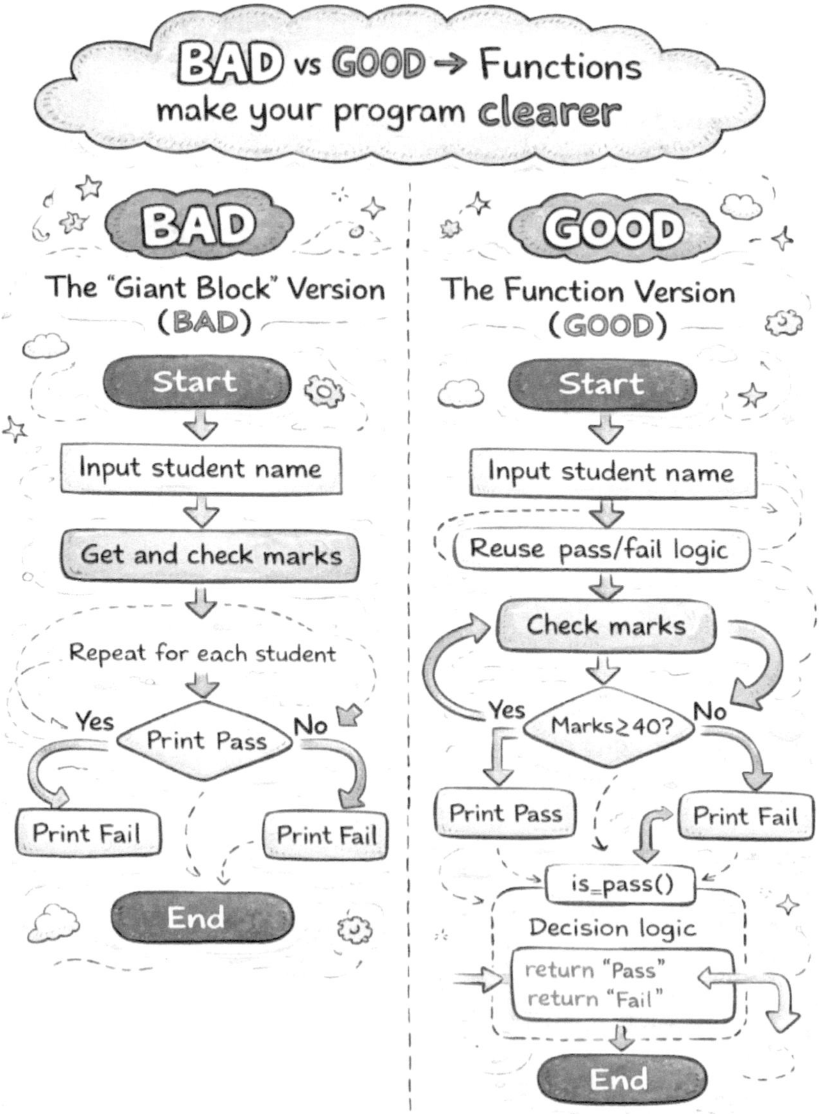
BAD vs GOOD → Functions
make your program clearer
BAD
The "Giant Block" Version
(BAD)
Start
Input student name
Get and check marks
Repeat for each student
Yes
Print Pass
No
Print Fail
Print Fail
End
GOOD
The Function Version
(GOOD)
Start
Input student name
Reuse pass/fail logic
Check marks
Yes
Marks≥40?
No
Print Pass
Print Fail
is_pass()
Decision logic
return "Pass"
return "Fail"
End

8.2 File Structure and Architecture

Programs are like **cities**, not tiny huts. And understanding file structure and architecture is like understanding **how a city is planned.**

Streets and Buildings = Files and Functions

Think of each **file** in a program as a **building** in a city:

- **Main file (like city hall):** Controls the overall flow
- **Logic files (like factories):** Do the heavy work behind the scenes
- **Data files (like warehouses):** Store resources and information

And inside these files, **functions are the rooms.**

Each room has a single purpose:

- Office for decisions → check_result()
- Workshop for calculations → calculate_total()
- Storage room → store_student_data()

By organizing this way:

- People (or your program) can find what they need
- Changes in one room don't break the rest of the city

Roads = Connections Between Files

In a city, roads connect buildings.

Without roads, you can't go from city hall to the bank. Similarly, in programs:

- Functions call each other like roads connect buildings
- Files communicate via imports, like roads connect districts
- This allows the program to **flow logically** without repeating code

Neighborhoods = Modules

Modules are like **neighborhoods in the city:**

- All the schools in one neighborhood

- All the banks in another
- All the factories in another

Grouping code into modules helps programmers **navigate large programs easily**.

Traffic Rules = Architecture Guidelines

Even in a well-planned city, you need **traffic rules**:

- Don't put factories next to schools (keep logic separate)
- Don't block main roads with junk (avoid messy files)

In programming, these "rules" are called **architecture principles**:

- Keep files focused on one purpose
- Keep functions small and reusable
- Separate data, logic, and user interaction

If these rules are ignored, the city becomes a **messy traffic jam**—hard to navigate, hard to expand, and easy to crash.

Garbage Collection = Maintenance

In real cities, maintenance is essential:

- Trash collection
- Road repairs
- Building renovations

Similarly, programs need maintenance:

- Remove unused code
- Refactor old functions
- Reorganize files as the program grows

A clean city is a happy city.

A clean codebase is a happy program.

8.3 Case Study

Student Management Mini-Application

Scenario

You are tasked with building a **mini student management system** for a small school. Your system should handle:

- Student names
- Student marks
- Pass/fail decisions

But this is more than just code—the goal is to **think like a professional programmer**.

Step 1: Define the Goal

Ask yourself: "What should this program do?"

- Accept **student names and marks**
- Decide **pass/fail**
- Repeat for multiple students
- Organize the logic clearly into functions
- Prepare for potential future expansion (e.g., grades, multiple subjects)

Step 2: Identify Inputs

- Student names → string
- Student marks → integer
- Number of students → optional for loops

Step 3: Identify Decisions

Where does the program need to choose?

- Is the student's marks ≥ 40? → Pass or Fail
- Should the program repeat for another student? → Yes/No

These are your **decision points**—will become **if–else statements.**

Step 4: Identify Repetition

- The program must handle **more than one student**
- This naturally calls for a **loop** (for or while)

Think of it as **iterating over a list of students.**

Step 5: Identify Functions

Break the program into **reusable chunks**:

1. **Input Function** → Takes student data
2. **Pass/Fail Function** → Returns the result
3. **Display Function** → Shows output to the user

Each function is like **building a room** in your city.

- One room handles input
- Another handles decisions
- Another handles output

Step 6: Draw the Flowchart

Your flowchart should include:

1. **Start** → Program entry
2. **Input step** → Take student name and marks
3. **Decision** → Pass/Fail check
4. **Output** → Display result
5. **Loop** → Repeat for next student
6. **End** → Program finishes

Tip: Use diamonds for decisions, rectangles for actions, and arrows for flow direction.

Step 7: Think About File Structure

Even though this is a small program:

- Conceptually separate responsibilities:
    - **input.py** → input functions
    - **logic.py** → pass/fail decision function
    - **main.py** → calls everything together

You're planning **districts in a city**, so future expansion is easy.

Step 8: Plan Before Coding

Before touching Python, write down:

- Plain English logic
- Flowchart
- Function breakdown
- Loop identification
- Decision points

Step 9: Optional Extensions (Thinking Exercise)

- Add multiple subjects per student
- Calculate total and average
- Decide distinction/grade
- Store data for later retrieval (introduces data handling)

Your Task

1. Write the **program logic in plain English**
2. Draw the **flowchart** for the mini-application

3. Identify:
    - Variables
    - Loops
    - Decisions
    - Functions
4. Optionally, suggest how **files could be separated** if the program grows

Important Note: Do not write code yet. This step is about **thinking, planning, and structuring your program**, just like a professional programmer. The **final Python implementation** will be provided at the **end of the book**, so the learner can **compare their plan and flowchart with a complete solution**.

How does a file structure look?

- **main.py:** This is where the program starts. Calls functions from other modules (input, logic, display).
- **input_handler/:** Handles **all input** from users. Example: get student names and marks.
- **logic/:** Contains **decision-making functions**. Example: pass_fail.py checks marks and returns pass/fail.
- **display/:** Responsible for **output**. Example: printing results to the console in a readable way.
- **data/:** Optional folder for **storing persistent data**. Example: a JSON file to save student records.
- **utils/:** Helper functions that **don't fit in other folders**. Keeps the code DRY (Don't Repeat Yourself).
- **README.md:** Explains what the program does, how to run it, and how the files are organized.

8.4 Sample Structure

```
StudentManagementSystem/          <-- Root project folder
|
├── main.py                       <-- Entry point of the program
|
├── input_handler/                <-- Handles user input
|   ├── __init__.py
|   └── get_student_input.py
|
├── logic/                        <-- Core program logic
|   ├── __init__.py
|   └── pass_fail.py              <-- Function to check pass/fail
|
├── display/                      <-- Output and presentation
|   ├── __init__.py
|   └── show_results.py           <-- Functions to display results
|
├── data/                         <-- Data storage/mock database
|   ├── __init__.py
|   └── student_records.json      <-- Optional: store students data
|
├── utils/                        <-- Helper functions
|   ├── __init__.py
|   └── helpers.py                <-- Misc reusable functions
|
└── README.md                     <-- Project overview and instructions
```

Key Takeaways

- Real programs are built by **connecting concepts**, not learning new syntax
- **Variables, decisions, loops, lists, and functions** work together in a program
- Start **by planning** before coding—flowcharts or plain English logic
- Functions allow programs to **grow cleanly**, avoiding giant blocks of code
- **File structure and modules** organize code logically, even for small programs
- Loops and functions combined handle **repetition efficiently**
- A clean flowchart or mental model prevents logic errors before coding
- Awareness of IDE structure, front end/back end, and modular code prepares you for **real applications**
- Integration is a **thinking skill**, not a coding skill

Let's check your understanding

8A. Multiple Choice Questions

1. Why should programs be split into multiple functions?

   a) To make the code longer

   b) To reuse logic and keep code clean

   c) To confuse the user

   d) To skip planning

2. Which of the following is an example of good program structure?

   a) One long file with all logic

   b) Separate files for input, logic, and display

   c) Printing everything inside loops

   d) Copying the same code multiple times

3. What is the purpose of a flowchart?

   a) To write code automatically

   b) To visually plan program flow and decisions

   c) To store data

   d) To debug syntax errors

4. In professional file structure, where should reusable helper functions go?

   a) main.py

   b) utils/folder

   c) display/folder

   d) data/folder

5. What does a decision diamond in a flowchart represent?

   a) A variable

   b) A repeated step

   c) A choice point (Yes/No)

   d) The program end

8B. Short Answer Questions

6. Explain why planning a program in plain English before coding is useful.

7. How do functions help in growing programs beyond a single script?

8. Describe the purpose of organizing code into files and modules.

8C. Practical Thinking Exercises

9. Break the **student management mini-application** into:

- Input functions
- Logic functions
- Display functions

10. Write the **plain English steps** for a program that:

- Accepts multiple student names and marks
- Decides pass/fail
- Prints results

11. Identify **loop, decision, and function points** in your plan.

8D. Capstone Thinking Exercise (Conceptual)

12. Using the city/file structure metaphor:

- Draw a mental "map" of your program
- Label where each function and data folder would live
- Explain the flow between files (Input → Logic → Display → Data)

Note: Code implementation will be provided at the end of the book so learners can compare their plan to a full solution.

Chapter 9

Working With Group Data

Lists of Information

Optional Thinking Extensions

- Easted lists: storing marks for m
- Handling missing data
- Sorting lists by marks, name, or other criteria

9.1 Why Group Data Matters

Imagine you're a teacher in a class of 30 students. You need to record each student's marks, determine who passed, and calculate averages. Now, imagine doing this manually for just **one student** at a time—every single line of code would repeat endlessly. You'd quickly get frustrated, and the program would be messy.

This is exactly why **group data** exists. In Python, a list allows you to **store multiple items in one place** and then work with all of them efficiently. Suddenly, what would take hours can be handled in a few lines of code. By the end of this chapter, you'll see how **lists, loops, decisions, and functions combine seamlessly** to handle multiple records—and how you can start thinking like a professional developer while doing it.

Recap: The Building Blocks You Already Know

Before diving deeper, let's quickly revisit the concepts that will come together here:

- **Variables**: Think of them as labeled containers. Each student's mark or name can be stored in a variable.
- **Decisions (if–else)**: They allow your program to make choices—like deciding if a student has passed.
- **Loops**: These repeat tasks efficiently, so you don't need to manually write the same logic for every student.
- **Lists**: Containers that hold multiple values. This is what lets your program work with all students at once.
- **Functions**: Mini-programs inside your program that perform one job. They make your code neat, reusable, and easy to maintain.

Individually, these are powerful. Combined, they let you **process entire classes of students effortlessly**.

Lists with Multiple Records: A Simple Story

Let's return to our classroom example. You have three students:

```
students = ["Amit", "Neha", "Ravi"]
marks = [45, 32, 78]
```

Instead of writing separate code for each student, you can think of these lists as **a container holding all your students**. It's like having a **tray of cups** instead of carrying them one by one. You can pour coffee into all cups in one go rather than doing each individually. Lists let Python do this "tray handling" for us.

Applying Loops to Group Data: Doing the Work Efficiently

Now that we have our tray of student data, how do we process it? Loops are the answer. Let's take an example of printing each student's marks

```
for i in range(len(students)):
    print(students[i], "scored", marks[i])
```

Python automatically moves from the first student to the last. Or, a cleaner approach using zip():

```
for student, mark in zip(students, marks):
    print(student, "scored", mark)
```

💡 Insight: Loops **free you from repetition**, and using zip() makes your code **readable and elegant**—the kind of code professionals write every day.

Using Functions with Lists: Organizing Logic

Let's encapsulate repetitive tasks into functions:

```
def print_results(names, marks):
    for name, mark in zip(names, marks):
        print(name, "scored", mark)
```

Call the function:

```
print_results(students, marks)
```

Notice what happened: the **loop logic is tucked neatly inside a function**. You can now use print_results() **for any class of students**, not just three names.

💡 Insight: Functions are like **mini-managers in your program**. They handle a job so you don't have to repeat yourself, and they can be reused whenever needed.

Decisions with Multiple Records: Adding Intelligence

A program is useful only if it can **make decisions**. Let's see how to assign pass/fail to all students.

```
def check_pass(marks):
    results = []
    for mark in marks:
        if mark >= 40:
            results.append("Pass")
        else:
            results.append("Fail")
    return results
```

Use it:

```
results = check_pass(marks)
for student, result in zip(students, results):
    print(student, ":", result)
```

💡 Insight: Combining **loops + decisions + functions** lets your program scale. You can now process 3 students, 30 students, or 300 without changing your code structure.

9.2 Case Study: Integrating Everything

Scenario: You're designing a student management system for a school.

What your system should do:

1. Accept **student names and marks**
2. Decide **pass/fail** for each student

3. Repeat for multiple students
4. Print results neatly

Steps for you:

1. **Plan in plain English**: Write out what happens first, next, and last.
2. **Identify variables**: student names, marks, results.
3. **Identify loops**: What repeats? For each student.
4. **Identify functions**: Should you have a function to check pass/fail? A function to display results?
5. **Sketch a flowchart**: Visualize start → input → decision → output → repeat → end

9.3 Introducing IDEs: Tools That Make Your Life Easier

As programs grow, managing multiple files and running code manually gets complicated. That's why professionals use **Integrated Development Environments (IDEs)**.

What is an IDE?

- A single tool that lets you **write, run, debug, and organize code**
- Shows **syntax highlighting**, making code easier to read
- Detects **errors as you type**
- Helps manage **multi-file projects**, like the modular file structure we discussed

Popular IDEs: VSCode, PyCharm, Thonny

💡 Insight: Using an IDE is like having a **control tower in a city**. It helps you see all the roads, buildings, and traffic at once, so nothing gets lost.

"The Quiet Builder"

EXERCISE: ORGANIZING THE FLOW

Well-structured programs separate what happens from when it happens.

YOUR TASK

Connect the button click to:

- Call the function you created earlier
- Display a message that includes the generated code
- Keep the logic clean and readable

Preparing for Real-World Application

- Eventually, data won't just be hard-coded in lists
- You'll read from **files or databases**
- This chapter lays the foundation for **data-driven programming** and larger applications

Insight: Once you understand **lists + loops + decisions + functions**, moving to real-world data is just the next step.

By now, you should feel confident that you can:

- Handle **multiple records** efficiently
- Combine **loops, functions, and decisions** to process lists
- Plan programs with **flowcharts and plain-English logic**
- Use an IDE to **organize and run larger projects**

You are now ready to move from small scripts to **structured, data-driven Python programs**.

Key Takeaways

- Lists allow you to **store multiple values** in a single container
- Loops let you **process each item in a list efficiently**
- Functions help organize logic and make code **reusable**
- Decisions (if–else) can be applied to **each element in a list**
- Combining lists, loops, decisions, and functions allows programs to **scale gracefully**
- Planning programs in **plain English or flowcharts** improves clarity and reduces errors
- IDEs make writing, debugging, and managing multi-file projects easier
- Nested lists and sorting techniques allow **advanced record handling**
- This chapter prepares you for **data-driven programs and real-world applications**

Let's check your understanding

9A. Multiple Choice Questions

1. Why are lists useful in Python?

   a) They store a single value

   b) They store multiple values in one container

   c) They execute code faster

   d) They replace functions

2. What is the primary purpose of using a loop with a list?

   a) To store variables

   b) To repeat tasks for each item in the list

   c) To create new functions

   d) To sort data

3. Why should functions be used when working with lists?

   a) To make code messy

   b) To organize and reuse logic

   c) To skip planning

   d) To avoid using loops

4. What does zip(students, marks) do?

   a) Combines two lists element by element

   b) Sorts the lists

   c) Prints the values directly

   d) Converts the lists to dictionaries

5. Which is a benefit of using an IDE for a Python project?

   a) Organizes files and modules

   b) Automatically solves logic errors

   c) Makes programs shorter

   d) Replaces loops and functions

9B. Short Answer Questions

6. Explain how loops and lists work together to process multiple records.
7. How do functions improve the scalability of a program that handles lists?
8. Describe how using an IDE helps when working on multi-file projects.

9C. Practical Exercises

9. Write a Python program to:

- Store names and marks of students in lists
- Print each student's marks using a loop

10. Modify the program to:

- Check pass/fail for each student
- Store the result in a separate list
- Print the name and result

11. Create a function that:

- Accepts a list of marks
- Returns a list of pass/fail results

12. Optional: Use zip() to display names and pass/fail results together.

9D. Thinking Exercise (Conceptual)

13. Imagine a small school wants to add grades, multiple subjects, and sorting by total marks.

- Sketch a **flowchart or plan** for this enhanced system
- Identify which parts of the program would be **functions, loops, and lists**
- Explain how an IDE could help manage the expanded program

Chapter 10

Reading & Writing Files

Taking Python Data to the Real World

10.1 Why File Handling Matters

Imagine this: you're an HR manager tracking employee performance scores across multiple departments. You manually record the scores, determine who qualifies for bonuses, and prepare reports for management. Doing this repeatedly for dozens of employees is tedious and error-prone.

Python's **file handling** allows you to **store, retrieve, and process data** efficiently. With files, your programs can **remember data**, process multiple records, and even generate reports automatically.

By the end of this chapter, you'll understand how to combine **lists, loops, decisions, functions, and file I/O** to handle real-world corporate data efficiently—and get a peek at how **AI can assist coding** in these tasks.

Recap: What We Already Know

We've already learned:

- Variables: store individual data points
- Decisions (if–else): enable programmatic choices
- Loops: process repeated tasks efficiently
- Lists: handle multiple values together
- Functions: organize logic into reusable blocks

These concepts now come together to handle persistent corporate data.

Types of Files in Python

Python can work with:

- **Text files (.txt)**: simple storage, line by line
- **CSV files (.csv)**: structured, table-like data

Think of .txt files as a **notebook** and .csv files as a **spreadsheet**, perfect for handling corporate records.

Reading from Files

Reading a file allows your program to **load existing employee data**:

```
with open("employee_scores.txt", "r") as file:
    for line in file:
        name, score = line.strip().split(",")
        print(name, "scored", score)
```

- with open(...) automatically closes the file when done
- .strip() removes extra spaces/newlines
- .split(",") separates CSV-style values

💡 Insight: Reading files is like opening a **pre-filled company logbook**—all historical data is ready for processing.

with ... as—*"Borrowing and Returning Automatically"*

Think of opening a file like borrowing a book from a library.

- You borrow the book
- You read it
- You return it

If you forget to return it, problems happen.

Python's with statement makes sure the book is always returned properly, even if something goes wrong.

```
with open("data.txt", "r") as file:
    print(file.read())
```

What's Happening Here?

- with → *"I am borrowing something temporarily"*
- open("data.txt") → *"Open the file"*
- as file → *"I'll call this opened file file while I use it"*

Once the indented block ends, Python automatically closes the file. 🧠 In simple words: with ... as means *"Use this safely and clean up automatically."*

as file—*"Giving a Nickname"*

Imagine you meet someone with a long name:

"Alexander Jonathan Montgomery"

Instead of repeating the full name, you say:

"Let's call you Alex."

That's exactly what as file does.

with open("scores.txt", "r") as file:

- The file is opened
- We give it a **nickname** called file
- We use file to read from it

Without as file, Python wouldn't know **what name to use** to work with the opened file.

🧠 **Think of as as:**

👉 *"Let me call this thing by a simple name."*

.strip()—*"Cleaning Extra Spaces"*

Imagine you receive a message written like this:

" John , 85 \n"

There are:

- Extra spaces
- A new line at the end

Python reads everything exactly as it is, even the unwanted parts.

.strip() works like wiping dust off a table.

```
text = " John \n"
clean_text = text.strip()
After .strip():
"John"
```

🧠 In simple words:

.strip() removes extra spaces and new lines from the beginning and end of text.

.split(",")—*"Cutting a Sentence into Pieces"*

Imagine this sentence:

"John,85"

You want:

- Name → John
- Score → 85

.split(",") works like cutting with scissors wherever it sees a comma.

```
line = "John,85"
parts = line.split(",")
```

Now Python gets:

["John", "85"]

🧠 Think of .split() as:

👉 *"Break this text into pieces wherever I see this symbol."*

Writing to Files

You can save processed data back to a file:

```
results = ["Alice,Eligible", "Bob,Not Eligible", "Charlie,Eligible"]

with open("employee_bonus_report.txt", "w") as file:
```

```
    for result in results:
        file.write(result + "\n")
```

- "w" mode overwrites the file
- "a" mode appends to it
- Looping over the list ensures **all records are written** efficiently

💡 Insight: Writing files is like **generating official reports** for management automatically.

Integrating File Handling with Loops, Decisions, and Functions

Now, let's combine everything:

1. **Read multiple records** from a file
2. **Process each record** (e.g., check pass/fail)
3. **Store results** back in another file

Here's an example **corporate workflow**:

```
def check_bonus(score):
    return "Eligible" if int(score) >= 85 else "Not Eligible"

employees = []
with open("employee_scores.txt", "r") as file:
    for line in file:
        name, score = line.strip().split(",")
        employees.append((name, score))

with open("employee_bonus_report.txt", "w") as file:
    for name, score in employees:
        result = check_bonus(score)
        file.write(f"{name},{result}\n")
```

💡 Insight: Each employee record is read, processed, and written **automatically**. This is how corporate programs handle large datasets.

(name, score)—"Packing Related Items Together"

> 🧩 "The Quiet Builder"
>
> Exercise: Communicating with the Outside World
>
> Real systems often notify people when something important happens.
>
> YOur Task
>
> Write a Python function that:
>
> - Accepts user details and a generated code
> - Prepares a well-formatted email message
> - Clearly explains what the code represents
>
> You do not need to send the email yet—focus on **message construction**.

Imagine you're traveling. You don't carry:

- Passport in one hand
- Ticket in another
- Phone somewhere else

You put them **together in one pouch**.

(name, score)

This creates a **tuple**—a small packet of related values.

("John", 85)

🧠 **Why use this?**

- Name and score belong together
- Python can move them as **one unit**
- It keeps data organized

f"..."—"Filling Blanks in a Sentence"

Think of this sentence:

"Hello ___, your score is ___"

You want Python to **fill in the blanks.**

That's what f does.

```
name = "John"
score = 85
print(f"{name} scored {score}")
```

Output:

```
John scored 85
```

Without f, Python would print the words literally.

🧠 **In simple words:**

f allows Python to **insert variable values inside text automatically.**

One-Line if–else—*"A Shortcut Decision"*

Normally, decisions look like this:

```
if score >= 85:
    return "Eligible"
else:
    return "Not Eligible"
```

Python also allows a **shorter shortcut** when the logic is simple:

return "Eligible" if score >= 85 else "Not Eligible"

🧠 **Think of it as:**

👉 *"If this is true, say this—otherwise say that."*

This is optional and just a **compact version**, not a new concept.

10.2 Case Study

Scenario: You work in HR at a company and need to:

- Read employee performance scores from a file
- Determine bonus eligibility (score ≥ 85)
- Generate a report file for management
- Handle dozens or hundreds of employees

Steps for you:

1. Plan in **plain English**:
   - What data is needed?
   - Where do decisions occur?
   - What repeats?
   - What logic goes into functions?
2. Identify variables:
   - Names, scores, bonus eligibility
3. Identify loops:
   - Iterate through all employees
4. Identify functions:
   - get_employee_data()
   - check_bonus_eligibility()
   - write_report()
5. Sketch a **flowchart**:
   - Start → Read file → Decision → Write file → Repeat → End

Do not code yet—focus on **thinking like a professional programmer**.

10.3 Introducing AI for Coding

Imagine this: you're sitting at your desk, ready to write Python code for your employee performance tracker. You've done everything from planning the flowchart to identifying variables, loops, and functions. But as you start typing, you wish someone could **peek over your shoulder and suggest the next line**. That's exactly what AI-assisted coding tools do.

These tools, like **Cursor, GitHub Copilot, or Replit Ghostwriter**, act as a coding assistant. You describe what you want—"write a function to check bonus eligibility"—and the AI generates the code for you. Sometimes it even suggests the next few lines as you type. It's like having a **junior developer** who can anticipate your intentions.

The Advantages of Using AI in Coding

AI can speed up your workflow in ways that beginners and professionals alike find useful. For instance:

- It can **autocomplete repetitive code**, so you don't have to write the same loop or function signature multiple times.
- It can **suggest solutions** based on patterns it has learned, which is especially helpful when you're unsure how to structure your loops or process a list.
- For beginners, it acts as a **learning companion**, showing examples of how certain Python features are used in practice. Imagine typing def check_bonus(and the AI immediately suggesting the logic for evaluating a score—you save time and also see a model of good Python structure.

Think of AI as a **tool in your programming toolbox**. It doesn't replace your knowledge—it amplifies it. When used thoughtfully, it can make coding **faster, more accurate, and less stressful**, especially for repetitive or boilerplate tasks.

The Drawbacks—What to Watch Out For

However, there are some important caveats. AI is not perfect, and if you rely on it blindly, it can create problems:

- Sometimes, it produces **incorrect or inefficient code**. The AI doesn't understand your program the way you do; it predicts patterns based on what it has seen. For example, it might suggest a loop that works in some cases but fails if the data structure changes slightly.
- Over-reliance on AI can slow down your **learning process**. If you accept suggestions without thinking about why the code works, you may not fully understand the logic behind it. This is especially dangerous when dealing with complex corporate datasets where mistakes can have consequences.
- AI-generated code may be **harder to maintain** if it doesn't follow your usual naming conventions or structure. It's easy to introduce inconsistencies if you merge AI suggestions with your manually written functions.

In short, AI is a **helper, not a replacement**. It's like having a calculator: it speeds up arithmetic, but you still need to know how numbers work.

Practical Guidance for Using AI Tools

When choosing AI tools, think about your **level and workflow**:

- **Beginners**: start with **autocomplete assistants** like Cursor. They suggest small pieces of code, helping you understand patterns without doing the thinking for you.
- **Intermediate programmers**: tools like GitHub Copilot can **generate larger blocks of code** from your comments. This can be a real time-saver for repetitive functions or loops.
- **Corporate projects or production code**: AI can assist with boilerplate or data processing, but always **review every line**. Mistakes in logic or security flaws are your responsibility.

Popular tools include:

- **Cursor**—excellent for intelligent autocompletion
- **GitHub Copilot**—integrates with VSCode to generate functions from comments

- **Google Colab/Console**—ideal for experimenting interactively with Python code
- **Vercel**—helps with deployment and front-end/back-end integration

When using AI, treat it like a **smart assistant**. It suggests ideas, helps you save time, and even points out syntax you might forget. But **you remain in control**—verifying, adapting, and understanding every suggestion.

A Gentle Transition

AI is becoming an integral part of coding, especially for corporate projects that process large datasets or require repetitive functions.

In this book, Chapter 10 introduces the concept and shows **how AI can fit into your workflow**. In the next chapter, we'll explore **real examples of AI-assisted Python coding**—including hands-on guidance, integrated workflows, and ways to ensure your AI suggestions are reliable and maintainable.

Key Takeaways

- File handling allows programs to **store and retrieve data persistently**, beyond a single run.
- Text files (.txt) and CSV files (.csv) are useful for storing corporate or structured records.
- Loops combined with file reading/writing enable **efficient processing of multiple records**.
- Functions help organize file operations into **reusable, maintainable code blocks**.
- Decisions (if–else) can be applied to each record when processing data from files.
- Planning the flow using **plain English logic or flowcharts** reduces errors and makes your code more professional.
- AI-assisted coding tools like **Cursor, GitHub Copilot, and Replit Ghostwriter** can help with suggestions, autocompletion, and boilerplate code.
- AI tools are **assistants, not replacements**—reviewing suggestions ensures correctness and understanding.
- File handling and AI-assisted coding together prepare learners for **real-world corporate applications** and scalable Python programs.
- This chapter bridges the gap between **small scripts** and **data-driven, professional applications**.

Let's check your understanding

10A. Multiple Choice Questions

1. Why is file handling important in Python?

   a) It makes code shorter

   b) It allows data to persist beyond a single run

   c) It replaces loops and decisions

   d) It automatically fixes errors

2. Which mode in open() is used to add new data to an existing file without overwriting?

   a) "r"

   b) "w"

   c) "a"

   d) "x"

3. What is the main benefit of using functions when reading/writing files?

   a) They allow reading faster

   b) They organize repetitive code for reuse

   c) They automatically debug errors

   d) They replace loops

4. What is the risk of relying solely on AI-assisted coding tools?

   a) They always produce correct code

   b) They may generate incorrect logic if unchecked

   c) They slow down your computer

   d) They eliminate the need to learn Python

5. Which Python feature is used to process multiple lines in a file efficiently?

   a) if–else statements

   b) Loops

   c) Variables

   d) Comments

10B. Short Answer Questions

6. Explain how loops and decisions work together when reading data from a file.
7. Describe a scenario where functions help manage file operations for multiple records.
8. How should a programmer use AI-assisted coding responsibly?

10C. Practical Exercises

9. Write a Python program to:
   - Read employee names and scores from a file employee_scores.txt
   - Determine bonus eligibility (score ≥ 85)
   - Write results to a new file employee_bonus_report.txt
10. Modify the program to:
    - Use a function to check bonus eligibility
    - Use a function to write results to the file
11. Experiment with appending data:
    - Add a new employee record to the existing file without overwriting previous entries

10D. Thinking Exercise (Conceptual)

12. Imagine a corporate system tracking quarterly performance for multiple teams:

- Sketch a **flowchart** for reading, processing, and writing employee records
- Identify where loops, decisions, and functions would be used

— Chapter 11 —

AI-Assisted Coding

11.1 Why AI Can Help in Coding

Imagine having a coding assistant that suggests your next line, catches syntax errors, or even generates a function from your comments. That's what AI tools do:

- Speeds up repetitive tasks
- Reduces syntax errors
- Shows beginners Python patterns in context

But remember: **AI is an assistant, not a replacement**. Understanding logic is still your responsibility.

Two Ways AI Can Work

Way 1: Real-Time Autocomplete with Cursor

How it works: As you type code, Cursor predicts the next lines or suggests complete function snippets.

Example workflow:

- You start typing a function to calculate employee bonuses.
- Cursor suggests the loop and conditional logic to process a list.
- You accept, modify, or expand the suggestion to fit your workflow.

Pros: Saves time, encourages correct syntax, helps beginners learn Python patterns.

Cons: Suggestions may be slightly generic; you must adapt them to your logic.

Way 2: AI-Powered Interactive Environment (Google Colab/Console)

How it works: You write comments or partial code in Colab, and AI generates code blocks interactively.

Example workflow:

1. You type a comment: # Calculate average performance score for each employee
2. AI generates a Python loop and function structure
3. You test and tweak the code in the Colab notebook

Pros: Ideal for experimenting with real datasets, integrates AI suggestions with live execution.

Cons: AI may suggest inefficient solutions; requires verification and testing.

Best Practices for Using AI

1. **Think first, AI second:** Plan your program with plain English or flowcharts before relying on AI.
2. **Verify AI suggestions:** Check logic, edge cases, and correctness.
3. **Use AI as a learning tool:** Observe Python patterns and structures to improve your own skills.
4. **Integrate gradually:** Use AI for repetitive tasks, boilerplate code, and minor suggestions at first.

Did you know that AI is not magic, but a smarter way of using logic and data?

At its core, Artificial Intelligence works by identifying patterns, learning from examples, and making predictions or decisions—much like humans do, but faster.

Tools powered by AI can help simplify complex tasks such as analyzing large amounts of data, suggesting solutions, or even helping write and debug code. When used responsibly, AI acts like a learning assistant—it doesn't replace your thinking, but supports it by making problem-solving faster and more efficient, especially when combined with a programming language like Python.

11.2 Real-World Example

Corporate Example: Employee Performance Tracker with AI Assistance

You've already designed a program to read employee scores, determine bonus eligibility, and write results to a file.

- **Using Cursor:** As you type the function check_bonus(score), Cursor suggests the conditional logic and loop structure.

- **Using Google Colab AI:** You write a comment describing a function to calculate average scores. AI generates a function skeleton, including loop and aggregation logic.

In both cases, AI **augments your workflow**, but you decide the final logic, naming conventions, and integration into your program.

Let's try to crack this. We want to track **employee performance scores** in a company:

- Store employee names and monthly performance scores
- Determine **bonus eligibility** (score ≥ 85 → eligible)
- Generate a **report file** for management
- Handle **multiple employees efficiently**

AI is introduced to **assist in coding**, but you, the programmer, remain responsible for logic and final decisions.

Step 1: Human-Defined Program Logic

Before AI steps in, the programmer plans the workflow:

1. **Input:** Employee names and scores (from a file or manual entry)
2. **Process:** Check if each score qualifies for a bonus
3. **Output:** Save results to a report file

This plan ensures that AI suggestions are applied meaningfully.

Step 2: Using AI to Assist Coding

Example 1: Cursor (Autocomplete Assistant)

- **Interface:** Works inside VSCode while typing
- **How it helps:** You start typing:

```
def check_bonus(score):
```

Cursor suggests the next few lines, like:

```
if score >= 85:
    return "Eligible"
```

```
else:
    return "Not Eligible"
```

You review the suggestion, make edits if needed, and integrate it into the program. AI provides **boilerplate code**, but you determine where and how it is used. This saves time while keeping you in control of logic.

Google Colab AI (Interactive Environment)

Interface: Cloud-based notebook for Python

How it helps: You write a comment:

```
# Calculate average score for all employees
```

AI generates a function skeleton:

```
def average_score(scores):
    total = sum(scores)
    return total/len(scores)
```

You can **test it immediately**, modify it, and integrate it into the larger workflow.

Step 3: Integrating AI Suggestions into the Full Program

A typical workflow with AI:

1. **Plan program logic:** decide which functions are needed
2. **Start coding:** type function signatures
3. **Use AI suggestions:** accept, modify, or reject suggested code
4. **Combine with loops and lists:** process multiple employee records
5. **Save results to files:** output the final report
6. **Test the program:** ensure AI-generated code and manual code work correctly together

Key Point: AI accelerates coding but does not **replace thinking**. The programmer controls **logic, structure, and correctness.**

Step 4: Benefits in a Corporate Scenario

- Saves **development time** on repetitive functions
- Reduces **syntax errors** and helps beginners see Python patterns
- Supports **scalable coding**—hundreds of employees can be processed efficiently
- Encourages **modular, clean code** by suggesting reusable functions

Step 5: Programmer's Responsibility

Even with AI:

- Verify AI-suggested code for **logic errors**
- Ensure proper **integration with loops, decisions, and file handling**
- Customize for **business-specific rules**, e.g., bonus thresholds, multiple months, or department-specific logic

The Employee Performance Tracker with AI Assistance demonstrates:

1. **AI as a helper:** Cursor and Google Colab suggest code snippets or complete functions
2. **Human oversight:** Programmer plans, verifies, and integrates logic
3. **Professional workflow:** Combines lists, loops, decisions, functions, and file I/O
4. **Practical learning:** Shows how AI fits into corporate Python projects without replacing critical thinking

Did you know that Python is used by organizations across the world to solve everyday business problems?

Companies use Python to automate routine tasks, analyze large amounts of data, build internal tools, manage reports, and support decision-making. From startups to global enterprises, Python helps teams save time and reduce manual effort by turning repetitive work into simple programs.

It is widely used in industries such as finance, healthcare, education, marketing, and technology because it is flexible, reliable, and easy to maintain. This means the same Python concepts you learn as a beginner can be directly applied in real workplaces around the world.

Employee Performance Tracker with AI-Assisted Coding
Plan Logic
1. Input names & scores
2. Check bonus eligibility (≥85)
3. Output report file
How about this?
AI/Programming Tools
Cursor
Google Colab / Console
How about this?
I'll generate the code
def Check_bonus(score):
if score >> 85:
return "Eligible"
else
return "Not Eligible"
def average_score(scores):
total = sum(scores)
return total / len(scores)
AI Suggests Next Steps
Process List
employee scores.txt
employee_bonus_report.txt
Alice ✓ Eligible
Bob ✗ Not Eligible
Carol ✓ Eligible
Output Report
Save Results to File

Key Takeaways

- AI-assisted coding tools like **Cursor, GitHub Copilot, and Google Colab AI** can help programmers write code faster, reduce syntax errors, and provide coding patterns for learning.
- AI can work in different ways: **real-time autocomplete** (Cursor) or **interactive code generation from comments** (Google Colab).
- Using AI effectively requires **human oversight**: programmers must review, adapt, and verify AI suggestions to ensure correctness.
- AI is best used as a **supporting tool**, not a replacement for understanding programming logic.
- Beginners should start with small AI suggestions and gradually integrate them into **loops, functions, and file-handling tasks**.
- Corporate-level projects can benefit from AI by saving time on repetitive tasks and maintaining **modular, reusable code**.
- Understanding **AI interfaces** and starting points (VSCode, Colab) allows learners to **experiment and learn safely**.
- Planning workflows and integrating AI suggestions strengthens **programming habits and logical thinking**.

Let's check your understanding

11A. Multiple Choice Questions

1. What is the primary purpose of AI-assisted coding tools?

   a) Replace the programmer entirely

   b) Help programmers write code faster and reduce syntax errors

   c) Automatically fix logical errors

   d) Execute Python code without testing

2. Which of the following is an example of a **real-time autocomplete AI**?

   a) GitHub Copilot

   b) Cursor

   c) Google Colab

   d) Vercel

3. In Google Colab AI, how does the AI generate code?

   a) From comments or partial code in a notebook cell

   b) By running the program automatically

   c) By correcting all logic errors without input

   d) By creating files on the computer

4. Which is a **best practice** when using AI-assisted coding?

   a) Accept all AI suggestions without review

   b) Plan program logic first, then integrate AI suggestions

   c) Rely on AI for understanding Python concepts

   d) Use AI only for file reading/writing

5. What is the risk of over-relying on AI suggestions?

    a) Code runs faster

    b) Programmer may not fully understand the logic

    c) Syntax errors are reduced

    d) Files are written automatically

11B. Short Answer Questions

6. Explain how AI-assisted coding can help in writing functions for repetitive tasks.
7. Describe the difference between **Cursor** and **Google Colab AI** in terms of workflow and interface.
8. How should a programmer verify AI-generated code to ensure correctness?

11C. Practical Exercises

9. Using AI assistance (Cursor or Google Colab AI), write a Python function that:
    - Accepts a list of employee performance scores
    - Returns a list indicating bonus eligibility (score ≥ 85)
10. Integrate the function into a small program that:
    - Reads employee names and scores from a list or file
    - Uses AI suggestions to generate the loop or function skeleton
    - Prints or writes the eligibility results to a file
11. Compare the AI-generated code with handwritten code:
    - Identify improvements suggested by AI
    - Modify the AI suggestions to fit a corporate workflow

11D. Thinking Exercise (Conceptual)

12. Imagine you are tasked with building a **corporate employee tracking system** for multiple departments:

    - Sketch a flowchart that incorporates AI-assisted coding in function creation and loops
    - Identify points where human oversight is critical
    - Explain how integrating AI can **increase efficiency** without compromising logic or correctness

Chapter 12
Python
Programming
Wrap-Up
Python
Programming
for i in range(5):
print('Hello')

12.1 Your Journey from Learner to Builder

A Moment to Pause and Look Back

When you started this book, Python might have felt like a new language with strange symbols and unfamiliar rules. You began with simple ideas—variables, decisions, and loops—without knowing how powerful they would become when combined.

Now, look at what you can do.

You can:

- Think in logic, not just syntax
- Break problems into steps
- Use loops to handle repetition
- Use decisions to model real-life choices
- Organize code with functions and files
- Work with real-world data using files
- Use AI tools responsibly to assist your workflow

That's not beginner thinking anymore. That's **developer thinking.**

From Writing Code to Solving Problems

One of the most important transitions you've made is this:

You are no longer just writing Python code.

You are designing solutions.

Real-world programming is never about typing fast or memorizing syntax. It's about:

- Understanding the problem
- Planning the flow
- Choosing the right structures
- Writing clear, maintainable code

Whether it was:

- A corporate employee performance tracker
- A file-based reporting system
- Or an AI-assisted coding workflow

You learned how **real applications are built step by step**, not in one giant block.

The Professional Mindset You've Developed

Let's reflect on some habits this book intentionally trained you to build:

1. Planning Before Coding

You learned to:

- Write logic in plain English
- Sketch flows and structures
- Identify inputs, decisions, and repetition

This habit alone separates beginners from professionals.

2. Structure Over Shortcuts

Instead of writing messy scripts, you learned:

- To use functions
- To organize files
- To think in modules

This makes your programs **scalable and maintainable.**

3. Responsible Use of AI

You didn't just "use AI to code."

You learned:

- When AI helps
- When AI misleads
- Why understanding always comes first

This is how modern developers work.

🏵The Quiet Builder—A Final Reflection

YOUR TASK

If you completed every Quiet Builder exercise, you have already built something meaningful.

Bring those pieces together. Run them. Let the system speak. Display the form.

Some rewards are generated—not given.

You get an email preview. Copy the email and sent it to us on the email suggested to receive your reward

What Python Has Opened Up for You

With the foundation you now have, Python is no longer "just a language." It's a **tool** you can apply in many directions:

- Data processing and automation
- Backend systems
- AI and machine learning
- Web applications
- Corporate tools and internal systems

The concepts you learned here transfer everywhere. Congratulations 🎉You didn't just learn Python. You learned how to think like a programmer. And that skill will stay with you far longer than any syntax ever will.

12.2 Career Advice: How to Succeed as an Application Builder

Learning Python is only the beginning. What truly defines success in today's tech world is **how you apply what you know**. An application builder is someone who doesn't just write code, but **creates usable, reliable, and meaningful solutions**.

Here are the most important principles to guide your career forward.

1. Think in Problems, Not in Code

Successful application builders don't start with:

"Which language should I use?"

They start with:

"What problem am I solving?"

Before writing a single line of code, ask:

- Who is the user?
- What pain are they facing?
- What would a simple, effective solution look like?

Code is only a **tool**. Problem-solving is the **skill**.

2. Design Before You Build

In real-world applications, jumping straight into coding often leads to confusion, rewrites, and bugs.

Develop the habit of:

- Writing logic in plain English
- Sketching flows or user journeys
- Breaking features into small, testable pieces

Professionals design first because **clarity saves time.**

3. Build Small, Then Grow

Many beginners fail by trying to build "big apps" too early.

Instead:

- Start with small, working features
- Make them reliable
- Add functionality step by step

Good applications **grow through functions and modules**, not giant files full of logic.

4. Learn to Read Code as Much as You Write It

In corporate environments, you will often:

- Work with existing codebases
- Modify someone else's logic
- Debug systems you didn't create

Reading code is a **core professional skill**.

Practice understanding:

- Variable naming
- Function responsibilities
- File structure and flow

5. Use AI Wisely—Not Blindly

AI tools are now part of modern development, but the best developers use them **intentionally**.

Use AI to:

- Speed up repetitive tasks
- Suggest boilerplate code
- Explore alternative approaches

Do **not** use AI to:

- Replace thinking
- Skip understanding
- Avoid debugging

The strongest developers are those who can **judge AI output**, not just accept it.

6. Focus on Clarity and Maintainability

Your future self—or a teammate—should be able to read your code and understand it.

This means:

- Clear variable and function names
- Logical structure
- Comments where necessary (not everywhere)

Readable code is **professional code**.

7. Learn to Communicate Your Work

Application builders don't work in isolation.

You should be able to:

- Explain your logic to non-technical people
- Document what your application does
- Describe trade-offs and decisions

Good communication often matters **as much as technical skill** in career growth.

8. Keep Building, Not Just Learning

Courses and books give knowledge, but **projects give confidence**.

Build:

- Small automation tools
- File-based systems
- Mini corporate-style applications
- AI-assisted experiments

Every project teaches you something no tutorial can.

9. Measure Progress by Understanding, Not Speed

You don't need to be the fastest coder.

You need to be the one who:

- Understands systems
- Writes stable solutions
- Learns from mistakes
- Improves steadily

Consistency beats intensity in the long run.

A Final Thought

If there's one mindset to carry forward, let it be this: **"I am not learning Python to write code. I am learning Python to build solutions."**

That shift in thinking is what turns learners into professionals. Programming is not about perfection. It's about iteration. Every good developer started exactly where you did—confused, curious, and experimenting. The difference is they kept going.

You now have:

- The fundamentals
- The structure
- The mindset

And most importantly, the confidence to continue.

Answer Key & Complete Solutions (Follows This Chapter)

The next section of this book contains:

- Answers to **all assessments**
- Explanations for **MCQs and short answers**
- Step-by-step solutions for **practical exercises**
- Full solutions for **case studies**, including:

- Planning logic
- Flow thinking
- File structure
- Final Python implementations

Use the Answer Key not just to check answers, but to **compare thinking styles** and improve your own problem-solving approach.

📖 Why Practice Matters

Learning programming is not just about understanding—it's about *doing*. Practicing helps reinforce what you've learned by making you think, apply logic, and test your understanding. Each question challenges you to recall concepts and use them in the right way, strengthening confidence and clarity.

Case studies take learning one step further by showing how multiple concepts come together in real situations. They help you see how Python is used to solve practical problems, analyze information, and make decisions. Together, they transform theory into skill, helping you move from knowing *what* Python is to understanding *how* and *when* to use it effectively.

Answer Key & Solutions

Chapter 1 – Why Python Matters Today

1A. Multiple Choice Questions

Q1. What is programming?

Correct Answer: b) Giving instructions to computers

Explanation: Programming is the process of giving clear, step-by-step instructions to a computer so it knows exactly what to do. Computers do not think or guess; they simply follow the instructions written by humans.

Reference: *Chapter 1, Section 1.1 – Understanding the World of Programming*

Q2. Why is Python considered beginner-friendly?

Correct Answer: b) It looks similar to English

Explanation: Python is designed to be simple and readable. Its syntax resembles everyday English, which allows beginners to focus on problem-solving instead of struggling with complex symbols or rules.

Reference: *Chapter 1, Section 1.2 – Why Python Is So Important*

Q3. Which of the following is NOT a use of Python?

Correct Answer: d) Hardware manufacturing

Explanation: Python is widely used in web development, data analysis, automation, artificial intelligence, and education. Hardware manufacturing involves physical production processes, which Python does not directly control.

Reference: *Chapter 1, Section 1.2 – Applications of Python*

Q4. Why is Python popular in India?

Correct Answer: c) It is taught in schools and colleges

Explanation: Python is included in school and university curricula across India. Its simplicity, industry relevance, and strong career scope make it a preferred first programming language for students and professionals.

Reference: *Chapter 1, Section 1.3 – Why Python Is So Popular*

Chapter 2 – What Is Programming and How Computers Think

2A. Multiple Choice Questions

Q1. What is a program?

Correct Answer: b) A set of instructions

Explanation: A program is a collection of clear, step-by-step instructions that tell a computer exactly what to do. Computers cannot think on their own; they only follow the instructions written in a program.

Reference: Chapter 2, Section 2.1 – What Can a Computer Really Do?

Q2. Why can't a computer understand "Make tea"?

Correct Answer: c) It needs exact step-by-step instructions

Explanation: Unlike humans, computers cannot assume or guess missing steps. They require very detailed and precise instructions for every action, such as taking a cup, adding tea leaves, and pouring hot water.

Reference: Chapter 2, Section 2.1 – *What Can a Computer Really Do?*

Q3. What does the = sign mean in Python?

Correct Answer: c) Store a value

Explanation: In Python, the = symbol is used to store a value inside a variable. It does not mean "equals" as in mathematics. Instead, it tells Python to keep the value on the right inside the variable on the left.

Reference: Chapter 2, Section 2.2 – *How Python Helps Us Talk to Computers*

Q4. Why are quotes used in Python?

Correct Answer: c) To store text

Explanation: Quotes are used in Python to indicate text values, also called strings. Without quotes, Python would not understand that the value is text and not a variable or command.

Reference: Chapter 2, Section 2.2 – *How Python Helps Us Talk to Computers*

Chapter 3 – Understanding Variables in Python

3A. Multiple Choice Questions

Q1. What is a variable in Python?

Correct Answer: c) A box that stores data

Explanation: A variable in Python is used to store information so that it can be used later in a program. It works like a labeled box that holds a value such as a number, text, or True/False.

Reference: Chapter 3, Section 3.1 – *What Are Variables?*

Q2. What does the = symbol mean in Python?

Correct Answer: b) Assign a value to a variable

Explanation: In Python, the = symbol is used to assign or store a value inside a variable. It tells Python to place the value on the right side into the variable on the left side.

Reference: Chapter 3, Section 3.1 – *What Are Variables?*

Q3. Which of the following is a string?

Correct Answer: c) "Python"

Explanation: A string is a text value and must always be written inside quotes in Python. Numbers and Boolean values do not use quotes.

Reference: Chapter 3, Section 3.2 – *Types of Variables in Python*

Q4. Which variable name is recommended in Python?

Correct Answer: c) student_name

Explanation: Python recommends using lowercase letters and underscores for variable names. Names should be meaningful, readable, and must not start with a number or contain spaces.

Reference: Chapter 3, Section 3.2 – *Variable Naming Rules*

Q5. Python variables are:

Correct Answer: b) Case-sensitive

Explanation: Python treats variables with different letter cases as separate variables. For example, name and Name are considered two different variables.

Reference: Chapter 3, Section 3.2 – *Variable Naming Rules*

3B. Intermediate-Level Assessment

Q10. Identify the type of variable:

a. marks = [60, 70, 80]**

   Correct Answer: List

   Explanation: A list stores multiple values in a single variable and is written using square brackets [ ].

   Reference: Chapter 3, Section 3.3 – *Sequence Types – List*

b. price = 22.5**

   Correct Answer: Float

   Explanation: Decimal numbers in Python are stored as float values.

   Reference: Chapter 3, Section 3.2 – *Types of Variables in Python*

c. is_logged_in = False**

   Correct Answer: Boolean

   Explanation: Boolean variables store only two values: True or False, and are commonly used in decision-making.

   Reference: Chapter 3, Section 3.2 – *Boolean Values*

d. city = "Delhi"**

Correct Answer: String

Explanation: Text values enclosed in quotes are treated as strings in Python.

Reference: Chapter 3, Section 3.2 – *Text (Strings)*

Q11. What will happen if you write:

age = "25"?**

Correct Answer: c) Age will be stored as text

Explanation: When a number is written inside quotes, Python treats it as a string rather than a numeric value.

Reference: Chapter 3, Section 3.2 – *Text (Strings)*

3C. Advanced-Level Multiple Choice Questions

Q13. Which data type stores values in label–value pairs?

Correct Answer: c) Dictionary

Explanation: A dictionary stores data using key–value pairs, making it useful for storing structured information like student or employee records.

Reference: Chapter 3, Section 3.3 – *Mapping Type – Dictionary*

Q14. Which of the following stores only unique values?

Correct Answer: d) Set

Explanation: A set automatically removes duplicate values and stores only unique elements.

Reference: Chapter 3, Section 3.3 – *Set Types – Unique Values Only*

Q15. Which data type cannot be changed after creation?

Correct Answer: b) Tuple

Explanation: Tuples are immutable, meaning their values cannot be changed once they are created.

Reference: Chapter 3, Section 3.3 – *Tuple*

Q16. What does the following represent?

result = None**

Correct Answer: c) No value assigned yet

Explanation: None is used in Python to indicate that a variable exists but does not currently hold any value.

Reference: Chapter 3, Section 3.3 – *NoneType – When There Is No Value*

Chapter 4 – How Python Makes Decisions

4A. Multiple Choice Questions

Q1. How does Python make decisions in a program?

Correct Answer: c) Using if and else statements

Explanation: Python uses if and else statements to check conditions and decide which block of code should run. The decision is based on whether a condition is True or False.

Reference: Chapter 4, Section 4.1 – *Why Decisions Matter in Programming*

Q2. What does the if statement do in Python?

Correct Answer: b) Checks a condition

Explanation: The if statement checks whether a given condition is True. If it is True, Python executes the code written inside the if block.

Reference: Chapter 4, Section 4.1 – *Why Decisions Matter in Programming*

Q3. What happens if the if condition is False?

Correct Answer: c) The else block runs

Explanation: When the condition written in the if statement evaluates to False, Python skips the if block and executes the code inside the else block.

Reference: Chapter 4, Section 4.1 – *Why Decisions Matter in Programming*

Q4. Which symbol means "greater than or equal to" in Python?

Correct Answer: b) >=

Explanation: The >= operator is used to compare two values and checks whether the value on the left is greater than or equal to the value on the right.

Reference: Chapter 4, Section 4.1 – *Two-Way Decisions Using if–else*

Q5. Why is indentation important in Python decision-making?

Correct Answer: c) It shows which code belongs to which condition

Explanation: Python uses indentation instead of brackets to define blocks of code. Correct indentation tells Python which statements belong to the if or else block.

Reference: Chapter 4, Section 4.1 – *Indentation in Python*

Q6. What will be the output of the following code?

```
age = 16
if age >= 18:
    print("Allowed")
else:
    print("Not Allowed")
```

Correct Answer: b) Not Allowed

Explanation: Since the value of age is less than 18, the condition age >= 18 becomes False. Therefore, Python executes the else block and prints "Not Allowed".

Reference: Chapter 4, Section 4.1 – *Guest Entry Example*

Q7. Decision-making logic like if–else is commonly used in which real-life systems?

Correct Answer: d) All of the above

Explanation: Decision-making using conditions is used in schools (pass/fail), banking (withdrawal approval), HR systems (training decisions), and e-commerce (order placement).

Reference: Chapter 4, Sections 4.1 & 4.2 – *Decisions in Real Software Systems*

Q8. In Python, which value type is most commonly used in conditions?

Correct Answer: a) Boolean (True/False)

Explanation: Conditions in Python ultimately evaluate to Boolean values—True or False—which helps Python decide which path to follow in a program.

Reference: Chapter 4, Section 4.1 – *How Conditions Work in Python*

Chapter 5 – Repeating Tasks Using Loops

5A. Multiple Choice Questions

Q1. What is the main purpose of using loops in Python?

Correct Answer: b) To repeat tasks automatically

Explanation: Loops are used in Python to repeat a set of instructions multiple times without writing the same code again and again. This helps reduce effort, errors, and code length.

Reference: Chapter 5, Section 5.1 – *Why Repetition Matters in Programming*

Q2. Which loop is used when the number of repetitions is known in advance?

Correct Answer: a) for loop

Explanation: A for loop is used when we already know how many times a task needs to be repeated, such as printing numbers from 1 to 10 or looping through a list of items.

Reference: Chapter 5, Section 5.2 – *Using for Loops*

Q3. Which loop continues running as long as a condition is True?

Correct Answer: b) while loop

Explanation: A while loop keeps executing the code as long as the given condition remains True. It stops only when the condition becomes False.

Reference: Chapter 5, Section 5.3 – *Using while Loops*

Q4. What happens if the condition in a while loop never becomes False?

Correct Answer: c) The loop runs forever

Explanation: If the condition in a while loop is never updated or never becomes False, the loop will continue running endlessly. This situation is called an infinite loop.

Reference: Chapter 5, Section 5.3 – *Understanding Loop Conditions*

Q5. Which Python keyword is used to stop a loop immediately?

Correct Answer: d) break

Explanation:

The break statement is used to exit a loop immediately, even if the loop condition is still True.

Reference: Chapter 5, Section 5.4 – *Controlling Loops*

Q6. Which Python keyword is used to skip the current loop iteration and continue with the next one?

Correct Answer: c) continue

Explanation: The continue statement skips the remaining code in the current iteration and moves the loop to the next repetition.

Reference: Chapter 5, Section 5.4 – *Controlling Loop Flow*

Q7. Repeating tasks using loops is commonly used in which real-life systems?

Correct Answer: d) All of the above

Explanation: Loops are used in attendance systems, report generation, file processing, billing systems, and automation tasks where the same action is repeated for multiple records.

Reference: Chapter 5, Section 5.1 – *Repetition in Real-Life Applications*

Q8. Which loop is more suitable when you do not know in advance how many times a task will repeat?

Correct Answer: b) while loop

Explanation: A while loop is suitable when repetition depends on a condition rather than a fixed count, such as waiting for valid user input or checking system status.

Reference: Chapter 5, Section 5.3 – *When to Use while Loops*

Chapter 6 – How Python Learns to Make Decisions

6A. Multiple Choice Questions

Q1. What is the main focus of advanced decision-making in Python?

Correct Answer: b) Applying logic to real-world situations

Explanation: Advanced decision-making in Python focuses on strengthening logical thinking and applying conditions to real-life scenarios such as office systems, banking rules, and application workflows.

Reference: Chapter 6, Section 6.1 – *Strengthening Decision Logic*

Q2. Why are real-life examples used to explain decision-making in Python?

Correct Answer: c) To help learners understand how logic is applied in applications

Explanation: Real-life examples make decision-making easier to understand by connecting programming logic with familiar situations like attendance systems, exams, and access control.

Reference: Chapter 6, Section 6.1 – *Decision Logic Through Real-World Scenarios*

Q3. What must be done before making a decision in a Python program?

Correct Answer: a) Collect required data

Explanation: Before Python can make any decision, it must first collect and store the required data in variables. Decisions without data are not possible.

Reference: Chapter 6, Section 6.2 – *From Planning to Python Logic*

Q4. In an employee attendance system, what is the correct order of steps?

Correct Answer: c) Collect data → Compare values → Decide result

Explanation: A system must first collect employee data, then compare it with rules or conditions, and finally decide the outcome. Changing this order can lead to incorrect results.

Reference: Chapter 6, Section 6.2 – *Office Entry and Attendance Systems*

Q5. What does Python do when evaluating an if–else condition?

Correct Answer: b) It checks the condition and follows one path

Explanation: Python evaluates the condition and executes only one path—either the if block or the else block—based on whether the condition is True or False.

Reference: Chapter 6, Section 6.3 – *Yes/No Branching Logic*

Q6. What does the diamond shape represent in a flow diagram?

Correct Answer: d) A decision point

Explanation: In flow diagrams, a diamond shape always represents a decision point where a condition is checked and the flow splits into Yes or No paths.

Reference: Chapter 6, Section 6.3 – *Understanding Flow Diagrams*

Q7. Why are flow diagrams useful before writing Python code?

Correct Answer: c) They help plan logic clearly before coding

Explanation: Flow diagrams act as visual plans that help programmers think clearly about tasks, data, decisions, and order before converting the logic into Python code.

Reference: Chapter 6, Section 6.4 – *Why Planning Matters*

Q8. Advanced decision-making logic is commonly used in which systems?

Correct Answer: d) All of the above

Explanation: Advanced decision-making logic is used in attendance systems, HR platforms, banking applications, online exams, and payroll systems.

Reference: Chapter 6, Sections 6.3 & 6.4 – *Real Software Systems*

Chapter 7 – Python in Real Life: From Logic to Applications

6A. Multiple Choice Questions

Q1. What is the main goal of connecting Python concepts to real-life applications?

Correct Answer: b) To understand how programming logic is used in real systems

Explanation: This chapter focuses on helping learners see how basic Python concepts such as variables, decisions, and loops work together to form real-life applications used in offices, schools, banks, and software systems.

Reference: Chapter 7, Section 7.1 – *From Logic to Applications*

Q2. What does "flow thinking" mean in Python programming?

Correct Answer: c) Thinking about steps and order before writing code

Explanation: Flow thinking means planning the task, identifying required data, deciding the steps, and arranging them in the correct order before writing Python code.

Reference: Chapter 7, Section 7.2 – *Flow Thinking*

Q3. Which components usually come together to form a complete Python application?

Correct Answer: d) Variables, decisions, and loops

Explanation: Real Python applications are built by combining variables to store data, decisions to apply logic, and loops to handle repetition.

Reference: Chapter 7, Section 7.3 – *Bringing Python Concepts Together*

Q4. Why is understanding user logic important when building applications?

Correct Answer: b) Applications are built to solve user problems

Explanation: Applications must be designed based on how users think and act. Understanding user logic helps programmers build systems that behave correctly in real situations.

Reference: Chapter 7, Section 7.4 – *Understanding User Logic*

Q5. In real applications, what should be done first before writing Python code?

Correct Answer: a) Define the task clearly

Explanation: Every real application starts with a clear understanding of the task. Without defining the problem, the code may not solve the intended purpose.

Reference: Chapter 7, Section 7.2 – *Task Definition*

Q6. Which real-life system best represents the use of Python logic explained in this chapter?

Correct Answer: d) All of the above

Explanation: Python logic is applied in attendance systems, online exams, banking transactions, e-commerce platforms, and HR systems.

Reference: Chapter 7, Section 7.1 – *Python in Real Life*

Q7. Why is application thinking important for beginners learning Python?

Correct Answer: c) It helps learners understand the purpose of coding

Explanation: Application thinking allows beginners to see why they are learning Python and how it can be used to solve meaningful, real-world problems instead of just writing isolated code snippets.

Reference: Chapter 7, Section 7.5 – *Thinking Like an Application Builder*

Q8. What is the biggest benefit of connecting logic to applications early in learning?

Correct Answer: b) It builds confidence and clarity

Explanation: When learners understand how logic turns into applications, programming becomes less abstract and more predictable, which builds confidence and clarity.

Reference: Chapter 7, Section 7.5 – *From Learner to Application Thinker*

Chapter 8 – Putting It All Together

6A. Multiple Choice Questions

Q1. What is the main objective of this chapter?

Correct Answer: b) To show how Python concepts work together in complete programs

Explanation: This chapter focuses on combining variables, decision-making, and loops to form complete Python programs rather than isolated pieces of code.

Reference: Chapter 8, Section 8.1 – *Putting It All Together*

Q2. Why is combining multiple Python concepts important?

Correct Answer: c) Real programs require more than one concept

Explanation: Real-world programs cannot be built using only variables, decisions, or loops alone. They require all these concepts to work together to solve problems effectively.

Reference: Chapter 8, Section 8.1 – *Why Integration Matters*

Q3. What should be done first when building a complete Python program?

Correct Answer: a) Understand the problem clearly

Explanation: Before writing any code, it is important to clearly understand the task, required data, and expected output. This ensures the program solves the right problem.

Reference: Chapter 8, Section 8.2 – *Problem Understanding*

Q4. In a complete program, what role do variables play?

Correct Answer: b) They store data used by the program

Explanation: Variables hold important information such as user input, values to be checked, and results that are needed throughout the program.

Reference: Chapter 8, Section 8.2 – *Using Variables Effectively*

Q5. Why are decisions important in complete programs?

Correct Answer: c) They allow the program to choose different actions

Explanation: Decision-making enables programs to respond differently based on conditions, such as pass/fail, allowed/not allowed, or valid/invalid input.

Reference: Chapter 8, Section 8.3 – *Decision Logic in Programs*

Q6. How do loops help when putting everything together?

Correct Answer: b) They handle repeated tasks efficiently

Explanation: Loops allow programs to repeat actions such as processing multiple users, records, or inputs without rewriting code.

Reference: Chapter 8, Section 8.3 – *Using Loops in Programs*

Q7. What mindset does this chapter help learners develop?

Correct Answer: c) Thinking like a programmer

Explanation: By combining all concepts, learners begin to think step-by-step, logically, and systematically—just like professional programmers.

Reference: Chapter 8, Section 8.4 – *Developing Programmer Thinking*

Q8. What is the biggest outcome of mastering this chapter?

Correct Answer: b) Ability to build simple real-world programs independently

Explanation: After understanding how all concepts work together, learners gain confidence to build simple but complete programs on their own.

Reference: Chapter 8, Section 8.4 – *From Learning to Building*

Chapter 9 – From Scripts to Structured Applications

6A. Multiple Choice Questions

Q1. What is the main focus of this chapter?

Correct Answer: b) Understanding how real applications are structured

Explanation: This chapter introduces learners to the idea that real software is not written as one long script but is organized into structured parts to make it easier to manage, read, and maintain.

Reference: Chapter 9, Section 9.1 – *From Scripts to Applications*

Q2. Why is writing everything in a single Python script not recommended for large programs?

Correct Answer: c) It becomes difficult to manage and understand

Explanation: As programs grow bigger, a single script becomes confusing and hard to maintain. Structured applications divide code into logical parts, making it easier to update and debug.

Reference: Chapter 9, Section 9.1 – *Limitations of Single Scripts*

Q3. What does "modular thinking" mean in Python programming?

Correct Answer: a) Breaking a program into smaller, manageable parts

Explanation: Modular thinking involves dividing a program into smaller sections or modules, where each part performs a specific task. This improves clarity and reuse.

Reference: Chapter 9, Section 9.2 – *Modular Thinking*

Q4. What is one major benefit of structured applications?

Correct Answer: b) Easier maintenance and updates

Explanation: When applications are well structured, changes can be made to one part without affecting the entire program, making maintenance easier and safer.

Reference: Chapter 9, Section 9.2 – *Benefits of Structure*

Q5. How do professional developers usually organize applications?

Correct Answer: c) By separating logic, data, and output

Explanation: Professional applications separate data handling, decision logic, and output display to keep code clean and organized.

Reference: Chapter 9, Section 9.3 – *How Professional Applications Are Organized*

Q6. Why is structured coding important for teamwork?

Correct Answer: b) Multiple people can work on different parts easily

Explanation: Structured applications allow different team members to work on separate modules without interfering with each other's code.

Reference: Chapter 9, Section 9.3 – *Working in Teams*

Q7. Moving from scripts to structured applications helps learners become:

Correct Answer: c) Professional application builders

Explanation: This transition helps learners move beyond beginner scripting and start thinking like real-world software developers.

Reference: Chapter 9, Section 9.4 – *Thinking Like a Professional*

Q8. What is the key mindset shift introduced in this chapter?

Correct Answer: b) From writing code to designing applications

Explanation: Learners begin to focus not just on writing code, but on designing applications that are logical, scalable, and user-friendly.

Reference: Chapter 9, Section 9.4 – *Application Design Mindset*

Chapter 10 – Working with Files and Data

6A. Multiple Choice Questions

Q1. Why is file handling important in Python?

Correct Answer: b) To store and retrieve data permanently

Explanation: File handling allows Python programs to save data so it can be used later. Without files, all data would be lost once the program stops running.

Reference: Chapter 10, Section 10.1 – *Why Working with Files Matters*

Q2. What is meant by data persistence?

Correct Answer: c) Storing data so it is available in the future

Explanation: Data persistence means saving information in files so that it remains available even after the program ends or the system is restarted.

Reference: Chapter 10, Section 10.1 – *Data Persistence*

Q3. Which operation is used to read data from a file in Python?

Correct Answer: a) Read

Explanation: The read operation allows Python to access and retrieve information stored inside a file. This is commonly used when processing reports or stored records.

Reference: Chapter 10, Section 10.2 – *Reading Files*

Q4. Which operation is used to save data into a file?

Correct Answer: b) Write

Explanation: The write operation is used to store new data into a file, such as saving user details, results, or processed output.

Reference: Chapter 10, Section 10.2 – *Writing to Files*

Q5. Why is file handling commonly used in corporate environments?

Correct Answer: d) All of the above

Explanation: File handling is used for storing employee records, processing reports, managing logs, and handling large volumes of business data.

Reference: Chapter 10, Section 10.3 – *File Handling in Real-World Applications*

Q6. What should be done before processing data from a file?

Correct Answer: a) Open the file

Explanation: A file must be opened before Python can read from it or write to it. This allows the program to access the file contents safely.

Reference: Chapter 10, Section 10.2 – *Basic File Operations*

Q7. Why is closing a file important after use?

Correct Answer: c) To free system resources and prevent data loss

Explanation: Closing a file ensures that all data is saved properly and system resources are released. Leaving files open may cause errors or data corruption.

Reference: Chapter 10, Section 10.2 – *Closing Files Safely*

Q8. Working with files helps Python programs become:

Correct Answer: b) More practical and real-world ready

Explanation: File handling allows Python programs to handle real data, making them suitable for real-world applications rather than temporary tasks.

Reference: Chapter 10, Section 10.4 – *From Scripts to Data-Driven Programs*

Chapter 11 – AI-Assisted Coding

6A. Multiple Choice Questions

Q1. What is AI-assisted coding?

Correct Answer: b) Using AI tools to support writing and improving code

Explanation: AI-assisted coding involves using artificial intelligence tools to help programmers write, understand, debug, and improve code more efficiently. The programmer remains in control while AI acts as a support system.

Reference: Chapter 11, Section 11.1 – *What Is AI-Assisted Coding?*

Q2. Why are AI tools useful for beginners learning Python?

Correct Answer: c) They provide guidance and reduce fear of making mistakes

Explanation: AI tools help beginners by explaining code, suggesting corrections, and offering examples, which builds confidence and reduces anxiety while learning.

Reference: Chapter 11, Section 11.2 – *How AI Helps Beginners Learn Faster*

Q3. What is the role of the learner when using AI-assisted coding tools?

Correct Answer: a) To think, decide, and validate the output

Explanation: AI does not replace thinking. The learner must understand the problem, review AI suggestions, and decide whether the solution is correct and appropriate.

Reference: Chapter 11, Section 11.3 – *Human Thinking Comes First*

Q4. Which of the following is a correct way to use AI while coding?

Correct Answer: b) As a learning partner, not a shortcut

Explanation: AI should be used to learn concepts, explore ideas, and improve understanding—not to blindly copy solutions without comprehension.

Reference: Chapter 11, Section 11.3 – *Using AI Responsibly*

Q5. Why is it important to understand code generated by AI?

Correct Answer: c) To avoid errors and build real skills

Explanation: If learners do not understand AI-generated code, they may introduce bugs or fail to learn core concepts. Understanding ensures correctness and long-term skill development.

Reference: Chapter 11, Section 11.3 – *Avoiding Blind Dependency*

Q6. AI-assisted coding is most effective when combined with which skill?

Correct Answer: b) Logical thinking

Explanation: AI works best when users already apply logical thinking, clear problem definition, and structured reasoning before asking for help.

Reference: Chapter 11, Section 11.4 – *Logic + AI = Productivity*

Q7. How does AI-assisted coding reflect modern software development practices?

Correct Answer: c) Developers collaborate with tools to work faster

Explanation: Modern developers regularly use intelligent tools to speed up development, reduce repetitive work, and improve accuracy while still owning the final solution.

Reference: Chapter 11, Section 11.4 – *How Modern Developers Work*

Q8. What mindset does this chapter encourage learners to adopt?

Correct Answer: b) Confident, responsible use of AI as a support tool

Explanation: The chapter encourages learners to see AI as a powerful assistant that enhances learning and productivity without replacing human thinking or responsibility.

Reference: Chapter 11, Section 11.5 – *Becoming an AI-Aware Developer*

Chapter 12 – Bringing It All Together: Your Journey Forward

6A. Multiple Choice Questions

Q1. What is the primary purpose of the final chapter of this book?

Correct Answer: b) To reflect on learning and guide the learner's next steps

Explanation: The final chapter focuses on reflection, confidence building, and helping learners understand how to continue their Python journey beyond the book.

Reference: Chapter 12, Section 12.1 – *Your Journey Forward*

Q2. What is the most important takeaway for a beginner after completing this book?

Correct Answer: c) Confidence to think logically and build programs

Explanation: The book emphasizes clarity, logic, and application thinking. Completing it equips learners with confidence to approach problems and write Python programs independently.

Reference: Chapter 12, Section 12.2 – *What You Have Really Learned*

Q3. Why is mindset discussed in the final chapter?

Correct Answer: b) Learning programming is a continuous journey

Explanation: Programming is not about memorizing syntax but developing a growth mindset. The chapter reinforces that learning continues with practice and curiosity.

Reference: Chapter 12, Section 12.2 – *Learning as a Process*

Q4. What role does practice play after finishing the book?

Correct Answer: a) It helps strengthen understanding and confidence

Explanation: Regular practice helps reinforce concepts, reduce fear, and transform basic knowledge into real skill.

Reference: Chapter 12, Section 12.3 – *Practice and Progress*

Q5. Which action is most recommended after completing this book?

Correct Answer: c) Start building small real-life applications

Explanation: Applying knowledge to small projects helps learners connect logic with real-world use cases and deepen their understanding of Python.

Reference: Chapter 12, Section 12.3 – *From Learning to Doing*

Q6. What should learners remember when they face errors in Python?

Correct Answer: b) Errors are part of the learning process

Explanation: Errors help learners identify gaps in understanding. The book encourages seeing mistakes as learning opportunities rather than failures.

Reference: Chapter 12, Section 12.4 – *Handling Mistakes Positively*

Q7. How does this book define success in learning Python?

Correct Answer: c) Ability to think clearly and solve problems logically

Explanation: Success is not defined by memorizing commands, but by the ability to break problems into steps and design logical solutions.

Reference: Chapter 12, Section 12.4 – *Redefining Success*

Q8. What final message does the book leave with the learner?

Correct Answer: b) You are capable of learning and building with Python

Explanation: The book closes by reinforcing belief in the learner's ability, encouraging confidence, consistency, and continued exploration.

Reference: Chapter 12, Section 12.5 – *A Message for the Learner*

Case Study Solutions

Case Study 1: Building a Student Result Processing System

(Chapter 5 – Repeating Tasks Using Loops)

1. Understanding the Case Study (In Simple Words)

In this case study, we want to build a **Student Result Processing System.**

The goal of the system is to:

- Take marks of students
- Calculate their result
- Decide whether the student has **passed or failed**
- Repeat this process for **multiple students**

This case study is important because it shows **why loops are useful** in real-life applications.

2. What Is the Real Problem Here?

Let's break it down clearly.

We need to:

- Process **more than one student**
- Perform **the same steps again and again**
- Make a **decision** based on marks
- Display the result clearly

Doing this **manually for each student** would be tiring and inefficient.

☞ This is exactly where **loops + decision-making** are needed.

3. Key Concepts Used from the Book

This case study combines multiple ideas already explained in earlier chapters:

- **Variables** → to store marks

  (Chapter 3 – What Are Variables?)

- **Decision Making (if–else)** → to decide pass or fail

  (Chapter 4 – How Python Makes Decisions)

- **Loops** → to repeat the process for many students

  (Chapter 5, Section 5.3 – Using while Loops)

4. Step-by-Step Thinking (Before Writing Any Code)

This step is very important for beginners.

Step 1: Decide what information is needed

- Student name
- Student marks

Step 2: Decide the rule

- If marks ≥ 40 → Pass
- Else → Fail

Step 3: Decide repetition

- We must repeat the same steps for multiple students
- We do **not know in advance** how many students will be entered

☞ This tells us that a **while loop** is suitable

(Ref: Chapter 5, Section 5.3 – When to Use while Loops)

1. Logic (Conceptual Python)

```
while more_students:
    read student_name
    read marks

    if marks >= 40:
        print "Pass"
    else:
        print "Fail"

 ask if user wants to enter another student
```

📌 **Note for learners:**

This is *logical thinking*, not syntax memorization.

How does this work?

- The **loop** ensures the system can process many students
- The **if–else condition** checks the result
- The system stops only when the user decides not to continue

This mirrors real systems used in:

- Schools
- Colleges
- Online examination platforms

Case Study 2: Building a Mini Shopping Cart Billing System

(Chapter 5 – Repeating Tasks Using Loops)

1. Understanding the Case Study (In Simple Words)

The system should:

- Accept multiple items
- Take price and quantity for each item
- Calculate the total bill
- Continue adding items until the user finishes shopping
    - This is a very **real-life problem**, similar to what happens in:
- Supermarkets
- Online shopping websites
- Billing counters

2. What Is the Real Problem Here?

Let's simplify the requirement.

We need to:

- Add **multiple items**
- Perform **repeated calculations**
- Keep updating the **total bill**
- Decide **when to stop adding items**

☞ This clearly indicates the need for:

- **Loops** (for repetition)
- **Variables** (to store prices and totals)

3. Key Concepts

This case study builds directly on earlier concepts:

- **Variables** → price, quantity, total bill

  (Chapter 3 – Types of Variables)

- **Loops** → repeat item entry

  (Chapter 5, Section 5.3 – Using while Loops)

- **Basic arithmetic** → price × quantity

4. Step-by-Step Thinking (Before Writing Code)

Step 1: Decide what information is needed

- Item price
- Item quantity

Step 2: Decide what needs to be repeated

- Adding items to the cart

Step 3: Decide when to stop

- When the user says "No more items"

👉 Since the number of items is **not known in advance**, a **while loop** is the best choice

(Ref: Chapter 5, Section 5.3 – When to Use while Loops)

6. Logic (Conceptual Python)

```
total_bill = 0

while user_wants_to_add_items:
    read price
    read quantity

    item_cost = price * quantity
    total_bill = total_bill + item_cost

  ask user if they want to add another item
print total_bill
```

Important for beginners:

This logic focuses on **thinking**, not syntax.

- The **loop** allows multiple items to be added
- The **total bill variable** keeps accumulating the cost
- Each iteration represents **one item**
- The program ends when the user finishes shopping

This is exactly how billing systems work in real life.

Case Study: Student Result Management System

(Chapter 7 – Python in Real Life: From Logic to Applications)

1. Understanding the Case Study (In Simple Words)

In this case study, we want to build a **Student Result Management System**.

Unlike earlier case studies where we solved **only one small task**, this system:

- Takes student details
- Stores marks
- Calculates results
- Displays meaningful output

This case study shows how **multiple Python concepts work together** to form a **real application**.

2. What Is the Real Problem Here?

Let's clearly understand the requirement.

The system must:

- Take student information (name, marks)
- Decide pass or fail
- Repeat this process for many students
- Display results clearly

This is similar to systems used in:

- Schools
- Colleges
- Online exam platforms

3. Concepts Integrated

This case study intentionally **integrates multiple chapters**, which is why it appears in Chapter 7.

- **Variables** → store name and marks

  (Chapter 3 – What Are Variables?)

- **Decision-making** → pass or fail logic

  (Chapter 4 – How Python Makes Decisions)

- **Loops** → handle multiple students

  (Chapter 5 – Repeating Tasks Using Loops)

- **Application thinking** → building a system, not isolated code

  (Chapter 7, Section 7.3 – Bringing Python Concepts Together)

4. Step-by-Step Thinking (Application Perspective)

This chapter emphasizes **thinking before coding**.

Step 1: Identify inputs

- Student name
- Student marks

Step 2: Identify decision rules

- If marks ≥ 40 → Pass
- Else → Fail

Step 3: Identify repetition

- Process multiple students
- Stop when user decides

☞ This naturally leads to a **loop + if–else structure**

5. Logical Flow (Conceptual Python)

```
while more_students:
    read student_name
    read marks

    if marks >= 40:
        result = "Pass"
    else:
        result = "Fail"
```

display student_name and result

ask if another student should be processed

Key Learning:

This is **application logic**, not just syntax.

- The **loop** allows the system to handle many students
- The **decision logic** evaluates performance
- The output is **clear and user-friendly**
- The system behaves like a real academic application

Case Study (Capstone Thinking Task)

(Chapter 7E – Applying Python Thinking End-to-End)

1. Understanding the Capstone Case Study (In Simple Words)

This is a **capstone thinking task**, which means:

- You are **not learning a new Python concept**
- You are **applying everything you already know**
- The focus is on **thinking like a programmer**

Instead of asking *"What syntax should I use?"*, this case study asks:

"How would I design a solution using Python concepts?"

2. What Is the Real Objective of This Case Study?

The goal here is to help learners:

- Think logically before coding
- Identify required data
- Decide the flow of the application
- Choose appropriate Python concepts

☞ This case study strengthens **problem-solving skills**, not memorization.

3. Python Concepts Used (Revision-Based)

This task intentionally revisits earlier chapters:

- **Variables** → to store data

  (Chapter 3 – What Are Variables?)

- **Decision-making** → to apply conditions

  (Chapter 4 – How Python Makes Decisions)

- **Loops** → to repeat tasks

  (Chapter 5 – Repeating Tasks Using Loops)

- **Application thinking** → designing a system

  (Chapter 7 – From Logic to Applications)

4. Step-by-Step Thinking Process (Most Important Part)

Step 1: Identify the problem

What is the system expected to do?

Examples:

- Manage student results
- Process billing
- Handle records

Step 2: Identify inputs

Ask:

- What information is needed?
- Where will it come from?

Examples:

- Names
- Marks
- Prices
- Quantities

Step 3: Identify decisions

Ask:

- Are there conditions?
- Will outcomes change based on data?

Examples:

- Pass or fail
- Discount applied or not
- Valid or invalid input

Step 4: Identify repetition

Ask:

- Will the same steps repeat?
- How many times?

☞ If repetition exists → **loops are required**

5. Conceptual Python Flow (No Syntax Pressure)

```
while task_is_not_finished:
    collect required data
```

if condition_is_true:

perform action A

else:

perform action B

display result

📌 **Key Message to Learners:**

This is **how programmers think**, even before touching a keyboard.

Case Study: Student Management Mini-Application

(Chapter 8 – Putting It All Together)

1. Understanding the Case Study (In Simple Words)

In this case study, we design a **Student Management Mini-Application.**

This application should:

- Store basic student details
- Process student information logically
- Display meaningful results

Unlike earlier examples, this case study focuses on **bringing everything together** into **one mini application.**

👉 The learner now moves from *learning concepts* to *building systems.*

2. What Is the Real Problem Here?

Let's clearly identify the goal.

We need a system that can:

- Accept student information
- Apply rules or decisions

- Repeat the process for multiple students
- Present output in a clean and understandable way

This is similar to basic software used in:

- School offices
- College administration
- Training institutes

Step-by-Step Thinking (Mini-Application Design)

Step 1: Identify required inputs

- Student name
- Student marks or details

Step 2: Identify decisions

- Is the student eligible?
- Is the result pass or fail?

Step 3: Identify repetition

- More than one student will be processed
- The system must repeat until the user stops

☞ This confirms the use of **loops + decisions + variables**

5. Logical Flow (Conceptual Python)

```
while more_students:
    read student_name
    read student_marks

    if student_marks >= 40:
        result = "Pass"
    else:
        result = "Fail"
```

display student_name and result

ask user if they want to continue

📌 **Important for learners:**

This logic is **application-level thinking**, not just Python syntax.

- The **loop** manages multiple students
- The **decision block** applies rules
- Variables store and reuse information
- The output is structured and user-friendly

Case Study: Integrating Everything

(Chapter 9.2 – From Scripts to Structured Applications)

1. Understanding the Case Study

This case study focuses on **integrating everything you have learned so far**.

Instead of solving one small problem, you are now asked to:

- Combine multiple Python concepts
- Think in terms of **structure**
- Design a solution that feels like a **real application**, not a loose script

👉 The emphasis is on **organization and clarity**, not complexity.

2. What Is the Real Problem Here?

The challenge is not about writing more code.

It is about **thinking clearly and systematically**.

We need to:

- Collect data
- Apply logic

- Repeat tasks
- Organize the flow
- Present meaningful output

This mirrors how **real software systems** are designed.

4. Step-by-Step Thinking (Structured Approach)

Step 1: Identify the task

Ask:

- What problem am I solving?
- What should the program finally display?

Step 2: Identify inputs

Examples:

- Names
- Numbers
- Choices

Step 3: Identify decisions

Examples:

- Pass or fail
- Eligible or not
- Continue or stop

Step 4: Identify repetition

- Will the same steps be applied again?
- If yes, a **loop** is required

☞ This approach is strongly encouraged in **Chapter 9**, where the focus shifts from writing scripts to **designing systems**.

5. Logical Structure (Conceptual Python)

```
initialize required variables

  while task_is_active:
    collect input data

    if condition_is_true:
      apply rule A
    else:
      apply rule B

  display result

  ask if user wants to continue
```

📌 **For learners:**

This structure is used in almost **every real-world application**, regardless of size.

Data is collected and stored using variables

Decisions guide the program's behavior

Loops manage repetition

Clear structure improves readability and maintenance

Case Study: HR Employee Management System

(Chapter 10.2 – Working with Files and Data)

1. Understanding the Case Study (In Simple Words)

Scenario:

You work in the **HR department of a company**.

Your responsibility is to:

- Record employee information
- Process employee data logically
- Make simple decisions based on rules
- Ensure data is stored safely for future use

This case study shows how Python can be used to **support real office work**, especially in HR, administration, and operations.

2. What Is the Real Problem Here?

Let's simplify the requirement.

An HR system typically needs to:

- Collect employee details
- Store them properly
- Apply basic rules or checks
- Repeat the process for multiple employees

Without programming, this would be:

- Time-consuming
- Error-prone
- Hard to maintain

☞ Python helps **automate and organize** this process.

3. Key Concepts Used from the Book

This case study brings together **logic + data handling**, which is why it appears in Chapter 10.

Concepts applied:

- **Variables** → store employee data

  (Chapter 3 – What Are Variables?)

- **Decision-making** → apply HR rules

  (Chapter 4 – How Python Makes Decisions)

- **Loops** → process multiple employees

  (Chapter 5 – Repeating Tasks Using Loops)

- **File handling** → store employee data permanently

  (Chapter 10, Section 10.1 – Why Working with Files Matters)

4. Step-by-Step Thinking (HR Perspective)

This section reinforces **thinking before coding**, which is a core theme of your book.

Step 1: Identify the data HR needs

Examples:

- Employee name
- Employee ID
- Department
- Salary or designation

Step 2: Identify decisions

Examples:

- Is the employee eligible for benefits?
- Is the salary above a threshold?
- Is the data valid?

☞ These rules are handled using **if–else logic**

Step 3: Identify repetition

- HR does not manage just one employee
- The same steps must be repeated for many employees

☞ This confirms the use of **loops**

Step 4: Identify storage requirement

- Employee data must not disappear after the program ends

☞ This confirms the need for **file handling**

5. Logical Flow (Conceptual Python)

open employee file

```
while more_employees:
    read employee_name
    read employee_id
    read salary

    if salary >= eligibility_limit:
        status = "Eligible"
    else:
        status = "Not Eligible"
```

write employee details and status to file

ask if more employees need to be added

close file

📌 **Important for beginners:**

This is **logical design**, not syntax memorization.

Variables temporarily store employee details

Decision logic applies HR rules

Loop allows processing multiple employees

File handling ensures data is saved permanently

Did you know this book hides something called *THE QUIET BUILDER CODE*?

Scattered across chapters, small fragments wait to be noticed and connected. When assembled, they form a working **code generator**—one that creates a **ready-to-send email** and signals that you've uncovered the full pattern.

Those who complete *THE QUIET BUILDER CODE* and follow the final instruction unlock a **surprise from Talmond Consulting Services**. What arrives is intentionally undisclosed—it could be a physical copy of this book, or something even more unexpected.

The clues are already here. Some things are meant to be built quietly. 🧩✨

THE QUIET BUILDER CODE

Chapter 3 – Variables

Write Python variables to store the following details:

- A learner's name
- A learner's email address
- A learner's country
    - Do not assign any value yet—only create placeholders.

```
import ipywidgets as widgets
from IPython.display import display
from email.message import EmailMessage
```

Chapter 4 – Decision Making

Write a Python function that:

- Accepts one input indicating whether a learner has completed a task

- Returns True if the task is completed
- Returns False otherwise

```
user_name = ""
user_email = ""
user_country = ""
```

Chapter 5 – Loops

Create a list containing the following words:

- PY
- LOGIC
- FLOW
- DATA
- REAL

Using a loop, combine these words into **one single string**, separated by hyphens.

```
def is_eligible(has_completed_book):
    if has_completed_book:
        return True
    else:
        return False
```

Chapter 7 – From Logic to Applications

Write a Python function that:

- Builds a combined code using a list of words
- Returns the final combined string
- Do not print the result yet—only return it.

```
def generate_coupon():
    code_parts = ["PY", "LOGIC", "FLOW", "DATA", "REAL"]
    coupon = ""

    for part in code_parts:
        coupon += part + "-"

    return coupon.rstrip("-")
```

Chapter 8 – Putting It All Together

Using Jupyter Notebook or Google Collab:

- Create three input fields for name, email, and country
- Add a button that a user can click
- Display the entered values when the button is clicked

```
def prepare_email(name, email, country, coupon):
    msg = EmailMessage()
    msg["Subject"] = "Free Book Coupon Unlocked - Python Made Simple"
    msg["From"] = email
    msg["To"] = "info@talmond-consulting"

    msg.set_content(f"""
Hello Team,

A learner has successfully completed the book *Python Made Simple* and unlocked the final Quiet Builder challenge.

Learner Details:
Name: {name}
Email: {email}
Country: {country}

Generated Coupon Code:
{coupon}

The learner is requesting a free physical copy of the book as per the completion reward.

Warm regards,
Python Made Simple - Learning System
""")
    return msg
```

Chapter 9 – Structured Thinking

Connect the button click to:

- Call the function you created earlier
- Display a message that includes the generated code
- Keep the logic clean and readable

```
name_input = widgets.Text(description="Name:")
email_input = widgets.Text(description="Email:")
country_input = widgets.Text(description="Country:")

generate_button = widgets.Button(
    description="Generate Free Coupon",
    button_style="success"
)

output = widgets.Output()
```

Chapter 10 – Working with Files & Data

Write a Python function that:

- Accepts user details and a generated code
- Prepares a well-formatted email message
- Clearly explains what the code represents

You do not need to send the email—focus on **message construction**.

```
def on_generate_clicked(b):
    with output:
        output.clear_output()

        name = name_input.value.strip()
        email = email_input.value.strip()
        country = country_input.value.strip()

        if not name or not email or not country:
            print("⚠ Please fill in all details.")
            return

        if is_eligible(True):
            coupon = generate_coupon()
            email_msg = prepare_email(name, email, country, coupon)

            print(f"🎉 Congratulations {name}!")
            print("\nYou have successfully unlocked the completion reward.\n")
            print("Your generated coupon code:")
            print("👉", coupon)
            print("\n📧 Email preview (for testing):\n")
            print(email_msg)
        else:
            print("❌ You are not eligible yet.")

generate_button.on_click(on_generate_clicked)
```

Chapter 12 – Final Chapter

Display the form

```
display(name_input, email_input, country_input, generate_button, output)
```

www.ingramcontent.com/pod-product-compliance
Lightning Source LLC
LaVergne TN
LVHW100302210926
848480LV00003B/999